The Billionaire Kitchen

A Private Chef's Culinary Journey

By

Chef Dana Minuta

Dedication

For Jean and Vincent

Acknowledgment

My journey has been nothing short of extraordinary, and it would not have been possible without the guidance, generosity, and support of so many remarkable individuals.

First and foremost, to my incredible husband—thank you for being my relentless source of strength, patience, and love throughout this journey. Your faith in me never faltered—even when I questioned myself. You stood by my side through every sleepless night, every rewrite, and every moment of uncertainty, offering loud encouragement and quiet support in equal measure. Thank you for being the carrier of my dreams. This wouldn't exist without you.

To my family—thank you for being the heart and soul behind my very first passion: becoming a chef. Your love, encouragement, and unwavering support have propelled me through every step of this journey. All of my first food memories were made in a loving home with you. From shared meals to shared dreams, you've nourished more than just my appetite—you've fueled my purpose.

To my inner circle of friends and my Brazilian Jiu Jitsu family from the blue basement and beyond— your steadfast support and encouragement have carried me through every chapter, every challenge, and every triumph— in life, in the kitchen, and on the mats. From devouring everything I've ever asked you to taste, to offering honest, thoughtful feedback, your belief in me has been my steady ground. You've been the soft landing when the world felt too hard, and I'm endlessly grateful.

To my cherished clients— you opened your homes and your lives to me, trusting me to nourish you and your families. The experiences we've shared at your tables have been the soul of this book. Thank you for your quiet elegance, your discerning tastes, and your resolute support.

To my beloved farmers, ranchers, fishermen, food growers, and producers—Thank you for your tireless work to provide us chefs with the best ingredients. Behind every dish, every detail, and every moment of grace is your dedication and boundless heart. This book, this journey, and every plate it inspires, is as much yours as it is mine. Thank you for feeding the world with integrity, care, and soul.

To my incredible coworkers who, like me, have chosen to serve the ultra-high-net-worth society: the yacht captains and crew, sous chefs, kitchen assistants, housekeepers, nannies, personal assistants, estate managers, personal trainers, security detail, architects, art curators, pilots, flight attendants, gardeners, groundskeepers, and every member of every family office —I'm beyond grateful for all the energy, passion, and teamwork you've contributed. Your hard work and dedication helped me bring this book to the table, and I couldn't have done it without you.

And finally, to every reader who holds this book in their hands: thank you. May you savor every story, every recipe, and every reminder that true luxury lies in intention, simplicity, love, and care.

With deepest gratitude,

Dana

Introduction

The book you're about to read marks the beginning of an exciting new series.

This first installment, *The Billionaire Kitchen*, serves as an introduction to my journey as a chef.

Within these pages, I share the experiences that shaped my path and ultimately led me to become a trusted culinary partner to some of the world's most notable billionaires.

The Billionaire Kitchen is filled with stories about food, travel, culture, adventure, and the lessons I learned along the way.

I'm thrilled to invite you into my world—to share both my stories and my recipes.

Future books in *The Billionaire Kitchen* series will shift the focus more toward the food itself—less storytelling, more recipes—offering a deeper dive into techniques and the craft of cooking.

I hope you enjoy this first book, and thank you for allowing me to share my story with you!

Preface

Before I ever set foot in culinary school, everything I knew about cooking came from books. I devoured cookbooks the way some people binge Netflix—page after page, recipe after recipe, picturing the aromas, the chaos, and the rhythm of a real kitchen. Like many chefs of my generation, one book changed everything: *Kitchen Confidential: Adventures in the Culinary Underbelly* by Anthony Bourdain. It wasn't just a culinary memoir—it was a revelation. Escoffier may have taught us how to cook, but Bourdain taught us how to *be* cooks.

Fast forward to 2014: somehow, I found myself training Brazilian Jiu-Jitsu with Bourdain himself. Yes—*that* Bourdain. The whole experience felt like stepping into a scene from one of his shows, only sweatier and with fewer cameras. What amazed me was how seamlessly his public and private selves aligned. The Tony on the mat was the same one from the page and the screen—sharp, kind, wickedly funny, and completely authentic. He had this effortless way of turning casual conversations into life lessons, usually delivered with the same dry humor he was famous for.

Food television blew up in the '90s, turning chefs into a new kind of celebrity. New York City kitchens became the epicenter of cool—places where ambition and adrenaline collided nightly. The people behind the line were the new tastemakers: creative, fearless, slightly unhinged, running on hangovers, caffeine and stubborn pride. But for all the attention, the pay didn't match the prestige. Behind the glamor, most chefs were still fighting to make rent.

Tony knew that struggle firsthand. Back when he was running Les Halles—a beloved French brasserie in Manhattan—he was making a respectable salary. Then life hit him with a $5,000 root canal.

"Dana," he told me, "I was basically married to my job, carrying all this responsibility, living in one of the most expensive cities in the world—and that root canal was literally going to bankrupt me."

I can't say for sure if that moment lit the spark for *Kitchen Confidential*, but it certainly fueled Tony's fire. He didn't just write about kitchen life—he exposed it. The late nights, the chaos, the madness, the dirty secrets, and the beauty of it all. He stripped away the polish and let the world see the grit, saying, in true Bourdain fashion, *"Here it is, world. Bon appétit."*

Bourdain's manifesto of honesty changed the game. Seemingly overnight, cooks stopped being invisible. Paychecks improved, benefits became a thing, and the entire culture began to shift—slowly, imperfectly, but in the right direction. All because Tony had the nerve to tell the truth about what really happened behind the kitchen doors.

Here's the thing about chefs: we're wired differently. Even the calm ones carry a quiet voltage, a hum that never shuts off. Outside the kitchen, the world moves in dull rhythms, but our minds spin—flavors, plating, the subtle twist that makes a dish sing. The hiss of a pan. The flash of oil. The heat of the flame. Kitchens are sanctuaries for misfits and dreamers, the ones who never quite fit anywhere else. You can be eccentric. Intense. Impossible. Even a hardened criminal. But if you can cook—you belong.

But the private chef world? That's a different beast entirely. It requires the passion of a restaurant cook and the grace of a diplomat. You have to be talented, intuitive, adaptable—and, at times, practically invisible. You're creating luxury behind the scenes, anticipating needs before they're spoken, and still finding joy in every perfectly plated dish.

Just as Tony showed an entire generation how to survive and succeed in the chaos of restaurant kitchens, I want to do the same for those navigating the private side of the culinary world—the kitchens of billionaires. There's no guidebook for that. Believe me, I looked.

We've now arrived at what I consider the ultimate culinary oxymoron: the rise of the "private chef influencer." The whole point of being a private chef is to be… well, *private*. So if you're thinking about pursuing a career in this field, I wouldn't suggest modeling yourself after the "YouTube private chef" crowd—because if you do, your career might end before it even starts.

Everything I know, I learned through a decade of trial, error, and occasional triumph. This book is my field guide—the lessons, the missteps, and the stories that shaped me for more than two decades. My path from bookworm to billionaire chef wasn't always smooth, but it's been one extraordinary ride!

About this Book

The Billionaire Kitchen is part cookbook, part memoir—a little bit recipe, a little bit revelation. I've written it as a timeline, so you can follow my journey as a chef and see how each experience shaped the way I cook. Some chapters include a single recipe; others have several. That's intentional. Because to me, the story behind the dish is just as essential as the dish itself.

I want to bring you inside the mind of a private chef—to show how we learn, adapt, and innovate without the safety net of a bustling kitchen brigade. It's about learning to swap ingredients on the fly, to build menus around personalities, moods, and moments, and to craft something beautiful from whatever the day brings. My goal is for you to cook these recipes with confidence, knowing that if you follow the techniques, they'll deliver every time.

For those who dream of following my career path, I hope to offer a clear-eyed look into the world of cooking for UHNW (Ultra High Net Worth) individuals—and how to navigate it with grace, precision, and a touch of flair.

For the billionaires and UHNW readers, you'll discover just how much intention, planning, and creativity go into even the simplest meal your chef serves. You may never look at a beautifully plated breakfast the same way again.

And for the everyday cook who just wants to elevate dinner at home—you'll find that great cooking doesn't require luxury ingredients or endless time. A little technique, the right produce, a sharp knife, and a generous helping of heart can turn any meal into something extraordinary.

Ultimately, I wrote this book to show that anything is possible with the right mindset. I'm proof that persistence, humility, and hard work can turn even the wildest goals into reality. It doesn't matter if you get knocked down nine times—what matters is that you stand up the tenth.

I hope *The Billionaire Kitchen* inspires you to feed yourself well, feed others often, and keep spreading the kind of love this world can always use a little more of.

Chapter 1
Yes Is the Answer.
What Is the Question?

For over two decades, I've lived in the shadows of the ultra-wealthy—cooking for those who move markets, own skylines, and rewrite the rules of power. The ingredients that have passed through my hands weren't just food; they were currency, traded in trust, taste, and discretion. I've worked for dynastic billionaires of the Northeast, self-made hedge fund magnates, real estate barons, and the Silicon Valley architects who built the bones of the Information Age. I've fed presidents and prime ministers, actors whose faces light up screens, designers whose names hang in closets worth more than cars, athletes, moguls, and the artists who give the world its soundtrack.

So why have you never heard of me? Because there's no address to plug into your GPS, no velvet rope to slip past, no critic waiting with a pen and a palate. Guarded gates conceal my dining rooms—and the architectural wonders within. The press doesn't get invitations. The only way to taste my cooking is to be invited inside—into the homes of my private clients.

When I got my start in the private chef world, it wasn't even recognized as an industry. The rules didn't exist. Not until 2010 did New York State pass the Domestic Workers Bill of Rights—the first in the nation—granting private chefs and household staff the same protections as corporate employees. Before that, there were no lines drawn between fair work and exploitation. The modern domestic worker carries a legacy older than the country itself, tracing back to indentured servants who labored until the job was done, bound by debts and contracts that left little room for choice.

In the 1600s, landowners and plantation barons needed cheap, steady labor to run their estates. They offered passage to America, a bed, and three meals a day in exchange for years of work—a contract disguised as opportunity. The servant would toil until the debt was paid, and freedom restored. But freedom always came with fine print. For centuries, not much changed. Private service was still governed by the old rule: he who has the gold, makes the rules.

I learned this lesson early. My first private kitchens were as much about diplomacy as they were about cooking. Every meal had to honor the taste and temperament of those who held the keys—and every decision had consequences. I quickly realized that the difference between a good private chef and a great one wasn't just skill with knives or flavor—it was intuition, discretion, and the ability to navigate a world where loyalty and trust were currency. In those kitchens, I didn't just learn recipes; I learned the unspoken rules, the politics behind every dinner, the invisible architecture of power that dictated every interaction.

I started cooking for billionaire families in 2002. At the time, there were fewer than five hundred billionaires on the planet. Today, that number approaches three thousand. Does that make me an expert on feeding billionaires? Some might say yes. I've certainly passed the 10,000-hour mark.

Even on a conservative estimate—fifty hours a week, forty-eight weeks a year—that's 2,400 hours annually. Multiply that by twenty years, and we're talking 48,000 hours spent in kitchens dedicated entirely to the ultra-wealthy. And that's a lowball—many weeks ran closer to eighty hours. Forty-eight thousand hours. Cooking for billionaires. Perfecting flavors. Reading rooms. Anticipating every desire before it's spoken.

20 years of menu planning

I never set out to be an expert in such a rarefied world. My goal has always been the same: to provide extraordinary food and hospitality while using my clients 'resources to support local farms, food growers, and producers. I feed my clients the way an Italian nonna feeds her family—early mornings wandering farmers' markets, hunting for the peak of flavor and ripeness in every fruit and vegetable, inhaling the scent of fresh herbs, sourcing the perfect cut of meat or the brightest, freshest fish. Back in the kitchen, I chop, stir, season, and taste with intention. Each dish is made with care. And just like Joe Pesci's character's mother in Goodfellas, I'll make a fresh meal for anyone who shows up at any hour. I bend over backward to accommodate schedules that could make most people dizzy, so my clients can maximize their time and maintain peak health. When it comes to running their kitchens, curating menus, and managing every aspect of hospitality, my mantra is simple: Yes is the answer. What is the question?

Most of my clients are household names. You've read their headlines—the divorces, the lawsuits, the escapades of their wild children, the running for public offices, the monumental successes and spectacular failures. You use their technologies, drive their cars, shop in their stores, listen to their music, watch their films, wear their clothing, and consume the products they've built.

I will not disclose their identities—past or present. This isn't just about NDAs. It's about respect. Discretion is the single most important ingredient in this business.

Cooking for another human is intimate. You cannot excel without care—for your guests, your team, your ingredients, and the farmers who produce them. Out of respect for my clients 'privacy, names and locations have been changed in this book. Unique stories that could identify them have been omitted.

I have stood in billionaire kitchens and watched world events unfold before they hit the news. I have held information I have never and will never share. I am a keeper of secrets, my hands never idle, always moving, chopping, stirring, tasting. My focus is constant: tending to my clients, protecting their privacy, and honoring my place in their homes—a contractual obligation to feed and nourish them, their families, friends, associates, and even their pets…all with a steady, accommodating smile.

Most people think billionaires live problem-free lives. They do not. My father used to say, "They put their pants on one leg at a time, just like I do." He was right—even if those pants cost more than most people earn in a month. When a client has a bad day—and believe me, they do—I soothe them with comfort food: the warmth of a roast, the smell of fresh bread, the quiet care in every bite.

I like to think of myself as a loving grandmother with a culinary degree. I keep the kitchen the heart and soul of the home, while never forgetting it isn't mine. The food I prepare belongs to my clients. I am fortunate to be trusted with feeding everyone lucky enough to get a seat at their tables.

Chapter 2
The Journey

People often ask me how I ended up cooking for billionaires. The truth is, it was never the plan. I grew up outside Newburgh, New York, where wealth was measured by whether someone's family had a cleaning lady twice a year.

As a teenager, I had big ambitions: I wanted to be a lawyer, then a judge, then the first woman president. That dream met its end the moment I stepped into my first business law class at SUNY Albany. What I found wasn't the courtroom drama of movies—it was paperwork, endless reading, and the kind of moral compromise that made my stomach turn.

Losing—and Finding—Focus

Freed from parental oversight, I did what most college kids do when they suddenly have no rules: I partied. Hard. SUNY Albany earned the ranking of number one party school in the nation while I was there, and I like to think I contributed to that achievement.

By the end of my freshman year, I was overweight from too many $5 beer nights, in debt from "free" credit cards handed out in the Student Center, and sitting on a 1.23 GPA. When I went home that summer, the disappointment on my parents 'faces was sobering. My father's work ethic is legendary—he's the kind of man who decided to "slow down" at eighty by only working five days a week. My mother's quiet disappointment cut even deeper.

My father's story always stayed with me. He came to America in 1956 by ship, just weeks after his father cancelled the Minuta family's original booking on the Andrea Doria—the one that sank off Nantucket. His intuition saved their lives. He worked relentlessly to give us opportunities, and I was squandering mine.

I decided that had to change.

That summer, I went back to work at F&J Pizzeria, the small-town Italian spot where I'd waited tables since I was fifteen. I started eating clean, running and lifting. I dropped twenty pounds . By the time I returned to Albany, I was fit, focused, and determined to turn things around.

I switched my major to Italian, with minors in business and philosophy. I got a job bartending and waiting tables at Quintessence, a diner-car restaurant near Albany Medical Center. The long shifts taught me discipline and how to read people—skills that would later prove more valuable than anything I learned in class.

My renewed drive pushed me toward new challenges. I tried out for the crew team and made it. The sport was demanding, but I loved it—the teamwork, the grit, the rhythm of early mornings on the river. My partner Leah and I went on to win many titles, including the New York State Collegiate Rowing Championship in 1999.

Rome and the Reconnection

By the time I graduated, I had rebuilt the life I had nearly thrown away. I earned my bachelor's degree in Italian with minors in business and philosophy.

In high school, I had been part of an exchange program in Arpino, Italy—a small hill town south of Rome that felt like stepping back in time. Studying there opened my eyes to a culture built around food, family, and slowing down long enough to enjoy both. Years later, I worked hard enough to return for a college semester abroad, reconnecting with my Italian friends—many of whom I still speak to today.

The only downside to all that dolce vita was that I picked up a cigarette habit—like every other teenager in Italy at the time. It stuck with me far longer than it should have, until I finally kicked it through hypnosis just before my fortieth birthday. Turns out the mind is stronger than nicotine when it decides to be—something I never would've believed back in my rowing days, when the only reward I wanted after a victory was a blue American Spirit.

Those months in Rome taught me more about life than any classroom ever could: how to savor, how to listen, how to live with intention.

"No, We Mean Next Week"

After returning to Albany, I stayed five extra months to finish my lease and save some money before heading to California for graduate school. That plan changed over a Quintessence brunch shift.

One Sunday, a few of my regulars—boat builders from the Port of Albany—came in for their usual brunch and a round of congratulations on my graduation. When they asked what I was doing next, I launched into my plan to move west for grad school— UC Berkeley, a master's in Italian, maybe even a PhD if the stars aligned. They laughed. Not unkindly, but the kind of laugh that comes from men who've seen enough of life to know when a twenty-something's plan is about to take a hard left turn.

"No," one said. "We mean next week."

They were delivering a brand-new wooden schooner, Adirondack II, from Albany to Chelsea Piers in New York City. They needed an extra set of hands. I'd never sailed a day in my life, but I said yes.

The delivery captain, Brad Stahl, was the kind of sailor who looked carved from salt and wind. Silver hair, steel-blue eyes sharp as the horizon, forearms roped with muscle from decades of hauling line. When he pulled on his yellow foul-weather gear, he looked like he'd stepped right off the Gorton's fish sticks box—only tougher. There was a calmness about him, though, the kind that comes from a man who's seen some shit and lived to tell about it. The kind of presence that makes even rookies feel safe.

The trip took eighteen hours. The Hudson River was familiar to me—I'd lived near it most of my life—but I'd never seen it from this vantage point.. The view was humbling. Forests gave way to cliffs, bridges, and eventually the shimmering outline of New York City.

When we docked, the owners of the boat, Rick and John Scarano, offered me a summer position as crew. Room and board were included. I was twenty-one, newly graduated, and broke. I didn't think twice.

A few weeks later, they asked me to manage the operation for the summer. I said yes again.

Summer 2000, sailing on Schooner Adirondack alongside Schooner Pioneer in NYC.

Lessons on the Hudson

That summer on Adirondack II was an education. I learned how to sail, how to manage a small business, and how to make charter guests feel like royalty. The pinnacle came with OpSail 2000, a historic event that brought over 120 tall ships and 40 naval vessels to New York Harbor.

That morning, thick fog hid the skyline. As it lifted, the masts of century-old ships rose beside modern skyscrapers. It felt like the past and present had collided on the Hudson. I knew I was exactly where I was supposed to be.

Then came the moment that truly set my future in motion.

Champagne and a Spark

One evening, a woman named Caroline Krug chartered the schooner for a private sail. Yes—that Krug. She arrived with cases of her family's Champagne and a catering spread from Dean & DeLuca.

The food was stunning—crudités, charcuterie, sushi, delicate tea sandwiches, and Vietnamese summer rolls arranged with artistic precision. The pairings were timed to each pour of Champagne.

As the sun dipped behind the city, the light bounced off glass towers and turned the skyline into liquid gold. The laughter, the clinking of glasses, the scent of the sea—it all felt enchanted.

When the guests disembarked, Caroline thanked the crew and left behind cases of Champagne and untouched trays of food. The captain popped a bottle, and we toasted as night fell over the harbor.

My first sip of Krug was transformative—bright, complex, electric. The summer rolls were a revelation: light, fresh, and somehow perfect with the wine. In that moment, I understood something I hadn't before. Food could be emotional. It could be an experience.

The idea of grad school disappeared. I wanted to live a life built around flavor, hospitality, and beauty.

Orphee III

Captain Greg Freitas, who ran the Adirondack II that summer, noticed my work ethic and my restlessness. He told me about a friend looking for crew in the Caribbean and thought I might be crazy enough to say yes. He was right. I had never set foot on a Caribbean island and had no idea what I was getting into—but I jumped anyway. A few weeks later, I was on a plane bound for the British Virgin Islands, ticket in hand and heart pounding, headed to join Orphee III—a 90-foot John Alden ketch built in 1938 for Ettore Bugatti himself.

Captain Mike, a British sailor in his sixties, lived aboard with his long-time girlfriend, Jan, who cooked for the guests. Mike was a recovering alcoholic who had traded gin for Tang. Jan was self-taught but talented, running the galley with quiet confidence. Together, they taught me the rhythms of island life—how to greet people, when to slow down, how to listen. And most importantly, tone down my New York attitude and get into the groove of island life.

Orphee III wasn't the newest, shiniest yacht in the Caribbean, but she had soul. She was all teak, brass, and history. My crewmate Scott, would become my work brother. He lived on island in a house on Magen's Bay with his roommate, Bubba, and Bubba's massive Bullmastiff named Tank. Off charter, Scott and I worked as deckhands, sanding and varnishing wood, scrubbing decks, fixing rigging, and polishing everything to a gleaming shine. On charter, I became stewardess, assisting Jan in the galley, making beds, cleaning heads, serving meals, and escorting guests on island excursions. Gender roles didn't matter—we each took on the work needed, a true team.

Our guests came for the beauty of the Caribbean, and we gave them just that. We anchored off Jost Van Dyke, swam in turquoise water, and danced at full moon parties on the beach. It was hard work and long hours, but I loved every second.

The Tang and the Gin

Our first charter season together was moving beautifully. Week-long charters, guests cleared through customs on Tortola, and sailing through the British Virgin Islands became our rhythm. Between excursions, we introduced guests to snorkeling, scuba diving, climbing Virgin Gorda's caves, and iconic stops like Foxy's, The Soggy Dollar, Willy T's, and the now-lost Bomba Shack, infamous for its full moon parties and psychedelic mushroom tea.

Then came the first 48-hour turnaround—the final push of the season. We would drop off the current guests on the east end of St. Thomas, steam back to Tortola to clean, refuel, and re-provision, all in time to welcome the next group flying into Beef Island.

When the first charter ended, the guests left in Red Hook with generous gratuities and promises to return. As planned, we headed back to Tortola—but Captain Mike was off. I initially chalked it up to exhaustion after a demanding week, until his behavior escalated: nearly colliding with moored yachts and clumsily docking at Road Harbour, communication broken, the hull scraped.

Once secure, Mike retreated to the engine room—but resurfaced hours later, shitfaced. The reformed alcoholic had fallen off the wagon. What followed was chaos: fights, shouting, and Mike physically shoving Jan, knocking her to the deck. Scott and I acted immediately—Scott pulling Jan to safety, me cornering Mike near the aft engine room, using every skill I had from bartending to de-escalate.

On the ladder, Captain Mike slipped, landed on his back, and I went to help. That's when I found the half-empty handle of gin. All day, he'd been mixing Tang with gin. I lost it. I confiscated the bottle, poured the rest into the harbor, and scolded him like the New Yorker I am. Mike exploded, creating a public scene at the fuel dock. Scott, Jan, and I packed our things, ready to leave, calling a taxi from the dock.

Eventually, Jan pleaded with us to stay for one final charter, knowing our absence would ruin her career. We agreed—but made it clear this was the last time.

The next morning, Mike had sobered and, against the odds, we pulled the yacht together before guest arrival. He was sheepish, grateful, but still visibly uneasy. Guests arrived—a famous Venezuelan family—and we sailed smoothly to Virgin Gorda. Scott helmed while Mike discreetly vomited over the stern. Thankfully, the guests never noticed. I made Mike a fresh glass of Tang and carried on serving.

After another night's sleep, Mike was himself again. The charter was a success, the guests generous with gratuities, and we had saved the yacht's reputation. But Scott and I had seen enough. Staying wasn't an option.

Graciously, Scott and Bubba offered me a sofa at their apartment in Magen's Bay while I planned my next move. Soon, I did: a final going-away party, and the next day, I flew to Key West—the land of schooners, sunsets, and conch fritters—ready for the next chapter.

Hauling up the sails on Schooner Adirondack, Summer 2000.

Vietnamese Summer Rolls

Yield: 16 rolls

Summer rolls have been in my repertoire since I started my career as a cook, inspired by the ones I fell in love with in New York Harbor after Caroline Krug's sailing excursion. I serve these often, substituting ingredients based on my client's preferences. These summer rolls call for nitrate-free smoked salmon, but you can easily substitute lox, cooked salmon, cooked shrimp, beef, chicken, or pork or make them fully vegetarian. I often make summer rolls out of leftover proteins, allowing me to repurpose delicious food that would otherwise go to waste.

Ingredients

For the dipping sauce/ Vietnamese vinaigrette:

• ½ cup filtered hot water

• 1 medium garlic clove, grated on a rasp-style grater

• ¼ cup honey

• ¼ cup freshly squeezed lime juice

• 1 tsp minced lemongrass, kaffir lime leaf or lime zest

• ¼ cup Vietnamese fish sauce or anchovy colatura

• 1 small hot red chili like Thai or Bird's Eye, minced (for less spice, other chilies can be substituted)

For the rolls

• 16 8-inch rounds rice paper

• 2 cups cooked rice vermicelli, rinsed and drained and lightly salted

• 1 cup shredded peeled carrots

• 1 cup julienned cucumber

• 1 cup firm-ripe mango, peeled and julienned

• ½ cup thinly sliced scallions

- ½ cup fresh mint leaves
- ½ cup fresh basil leaves
- ½ cup fresh cilantro leaves
- 1 firm-ripe avocado, sliced into 16 pieces
- 8 oz nitrate-free smoked salmon

Directions

1. Make the dipping sauce: Grate the fresh garlic into a medium-sized bowl. Add the honey, pour in the hot water, and whisk until the mixture is homogeneous. Add the remaining ingredients and set aside until needed.

2. Fill a large bowl or pie pan large enough to accommodate the rice paper with hot water. Dip a sheet of rice paper into the bowl for a few seconds until the rice paper is pliable, but not too soft. Lay it on a damp towel.

3. Lay a slice of smoked salmon and an avocado slice onto the lower third of the rice paper. Spread some of the noodles, carrots, cucumber, mango, scallion, and herbs over the salmon and avocado. Fold up the bottom edge to cover, then fold in the sides. Roll tightly and transfer to a plate or tray lined with a damp towel. Cover with another damp towel and repeat the process with the remaining fifteen rolls.

4. To serve, slice each roll in half with a very sharp knife, plate, and serve with dipping sauce. Rolls can also be made a few hours in advance, stored in the refrigerator covered with damp towels and slices just before serving.

Chapter 3
Synchronicity

My time in Key West was short-lived. I'd been hired as a deckhand on Schooner America, a replica of the 139-foot yacht that won the Royal Yacht Squadron's 100 Guinea Cup in 1851. This version was built by Scarano Boat Building in Albany—the same shipwrights who built my first schooner, Adirondack. I'd bonded with the America crew during OpSail 2000, and they were thrilled to bring me aboard. Some of those friendships have survived to this day.

I knew a drug test was coming—America was a US Coast Guard–certified vessel. I'd smoked a little reefer with Scott and Bubba not even a month earlier (as one does in the Caribbean), so I launched into a cleanse, deploying every trick my college buddies swore would work.

It didn't. I failed.

Today, with cannabis legal in most of the country, it might not have mattered. Back then, it was a career-ender. And since part of the compensation was a bunk onboard, failing the test meant I wasn't just jobless—I was homeless in Key West. I tried bartending, but I couldn't afford rent. My last dollars evaporated on a week in a cheap hotel after being kicked off the boat. I finally called my parents in New York, begging for help to get home. They agreed, but the disappointment was palpable.

Rock Bottom, Rebooted

Humiliated and humbled, I retreated to New York's Hudson Valley in the dead of winter, moving back into my childhood home. With my bachelor's degree, I qualified to substitute teach in the Newburgh school district. I took the gig while staying in touch with my old captains, hoping for any opening back on the water. Meanwhile, substitute teaching eighth graders was soul-sucking.

Salvation arrived in the form of a phone call from Captain Steve, one of my mentors from Adirondack. He knew a captain seeking crew to deliver a Swan 57 from Antigua to Baltimore. No contract tied me to the school district, so I jumped at it. In my mind, a thousand miles of open ocean was safer than a classroom full of teenagers in Newburgh—the crime capital of New York State.

Baptism by Saltwater

S/Y Synchronicity was my first real leap into the unknown—my first offshore delivery. I didn't know Captain Frank, but Captain Steve's word carried weight with me, so I trusted it. At the airport, I nursed nerves with Mount Gay rum and club sodas, talking to strangers like we'd known each other for years. By the time I boarded, the buzz wrapped me like a blanket. I passed out and woke to the humid, familiar embrace of Caribbean air—the kind that fills your lungs and tells you you're alive.

Truth was, I was green. I'd sailed, sure—but never days from land, never in the deep water where there's no turning back. Surrounded by real sailors—men with sun-carved faces and stories that smelled of salt and diesel—I offered the one thing I knew I could give: food. Cooking felt like currency—my way of earning my keep and covering for the minor detail that I was wildly unqualified to be getting paid as an offshore sailor.

Good Luck and Superstition

Captain Frank and I went to the local island market to provision the yacht for our delivery. We filled three carts with whatever we could scavenge. Supplies were limited—just frozen island-raised meat with handwritten labels curling at the edges: beef, lamb, goat, chicken. Nothing familiar, nothing packaged, nothing safe. I decided to cook what I knew—simple one-pot meals with heart: Thai curry, Chicken Parmesan, my mother's Boeuf Bourguignon, a taste of home for when the ocean swallowed us whole.

We stowed provisions, cast off, and the harbor fell behind us. I stood at the stern and let Antigua imprint itself on me—emerald mountains rising from impossibly blue water. It hit me how surreal it was that this was my life again—salt, wind, sunlight, waves—not fluorescent lights and cinder blocks in a Newburgh classroom that felt like slow death.

Sailors cling to superstition the way drowning men cling to driftwood. So when Captain Frank laughed and called me the "good luck charm," I let myself believe it. The seas were kind—15 knots from the northeast, a clean beam reach off our starboard side. A gift. A blessing. A promise. If the wind stayed with us, we could ride that line to Baltimore for a week straight, barely adjusting a sail.

Frank's plan was simple: sail as long as the wind allowed. Use the motor only to feed the batteries or if the air abandoned us.

The Religion of the Sea

I'd devoured enough sea narratives to know calamity tends to clock in around 2 a.m. So the night watch rotation—two crew at a time—felt like a lifeline. Four on, eight off during the day; at night, four on, four off, a rhythm that became our heartbeat. Enough rest to stay sharp. Enough time for me to cook, to nurture, to do the one thing that tethered me to myself.

I thought I'd sleep deeply in the off-hours, but the ocean electrified me. The boat sliced through moonlit water and something ancient in me woke up. Adrenaline surged. When I finally slept, I slept like I'd left my body behind—dreams vivid, wild, as if the ocean was rearranging my subconscious.

Most people will never know the disorienting beauty of being a speck in the middle of the Atlantic—no land, no landmarks, no proof the world exists beyond the horizon. Just sea. Sky. The thin line where they touch. Dolphins racing our bow, stitching joy into the monotony. And, sometimes, a ghostly cargo ship carving through the distance like a passing planet. I discovered that offshore sailing has one unexpected superpower: it introduces you to your own soul. It leaves a strange, unexpected spirituality clinging to you long after you've stepped off the boat.

The Wrong Captain Frank

When land finally revealed itself after eight days, it felt unreal—like an hallucination resolving into coastline. We approached Norfolk, Virginia, expecting to glide through customs without a hitch, before continuing north through the Chesapeake toward Baltimore—our final destination.

Captain Frank brought the yacht into the customs dock with the kind of cool, surgical precision that made me wonder if he'd practiced autopilot landings in a past life. A squad of uniformed agents was waiting for us, looking like they'd been rehearsing their "We'll be conducting a thorough inspection" line in the mirror all morning. We were ordered off the boat and onto the dock—no arguments, no eye contact…nothing.

We'd already begun "company's coming" cleanup mode on the way in: two double-bagged contractor sacks of garbage sitting front and center on the bow like twin hood ornaments of shame. All we wanted was to get checked in, shove off, and make Baltimore before sunset. Thirty minutes, tops—or so we thought. Somehow, hours evaporated.

From the dock, we listened to thuds, bangs, and the unmistakable sound of cabinetry being treated like it owed somebody money. Whatever those agents were looking for, they were hunting with enthusiasm. I asked Captain Frank if this was normal. One look at his face told me it wasn't—and also that I should shut up immediately.

Two agents eventually appeared topside, summoned the captain, and he boarded like a man walking into his own execution. Stoic. Silent. Fully aware that whatever was happening below, it wasn't a birthday party.

My heart was doing burpees. Had we unknowingly smuggled something? Drugs? Firearms? An illegal houseplant? If there was contraband, would my ignorance spare me—or would I be explaining myself to a judge who didn't care that prison was never part of my life plan?

After a nauseating eternity, the agents resurfaced, snapped off their latex gloves like post-surgery doctors, and thanked us for our patience. They hadn't brought a dog, hadn't checked the giant garbage bags sitting right under their noses, and yet—just like that— we were cleared to re-enter the United States of America. God bless efficiency.

Imprisonment Dodged, Story Earned

Engines on. Lines off. We pointed the bow north and got moving fast enough for Captain Frank to visibly exhale. "Dana, can you start putting this place back together?" he asked, which is boat-speak for I can't look at that disaster zone for one more second.

Below deck looked like a hurricane had discovered espresso martinis. Every cabinet emptied, every cushion flipped, every floorboard lifted. If a stone had existed, they'd unturned it, interrogated it, and frisked it twice. It took me over an hour to restore order. When the space finally resembled a yacht again instead of a crime scene, I popped my head up.

"Anyone hungry?" I asked.

"You got any more of that beef stew? What'd you call it— Bouefff Bourgig-non-non-non?" Captain Frank purposely butchering the French with a big grin.

"Coming right up, Captain," I said, stupidly proud.

We sat in the cockpit eating the last of the Boeuf Bourguignon made with Antiguan beef, grateful customs hadn't forced us to ditch the fridge's contents. The sky dusted itself in dusk as Baltimore rose ahead of us in silhouette.

"Captain Frank, can I ask a question?" I said.

He laughed. "Dana, you have a question? Color me shocked. Shoot."

"Why did they tear the boat apart? Does that always happen coming back into the States?"

He grinned. "No, Dana. Not normal. Turns out there's another captain with my exact name—first and last—who's a notorious drug-runner. Apparently, he's made quite a name for himself. Thankfully, this yacht didn't match the kind of boats that Captain Frank uses. But they had to be sure. Could've been worse—they didn't slice cushions or open bulkheads. That's... what we call a lucky day."

We reached the marina in Baltimore, tied off, and just like that— my first offshore delivery was in the books.

Boeuf Bourgogne

Yield: 6 servings

Ingredients

• 6 oz nitrate-free bacon, cut into lardons (1/4 inch thick by 1-1 1/2 inches long)

• 3 pounds of pasture-raised stewing beef, cut into cubes

• 1 medium diced onion

• 1 medium diced carrot

• 1 Kosher sea salt

• 2 TB flour

• 3 cups of full-bodied young Burgundy or similar red wine

• 2-3 cups beef stock or homemade brown chicken stock

• 1 TB tomato paste

• 2 cloves garlic, grated on a rasp-style grater

• 3 fresh thyme sprigs

• 1 bay leaf

• 1 pound of peeled small white pearl onions

• 1-½ TB unsalted butter

• 1-½ TB avocado oil

• 1 pound of quartered fresh mushrooms

• 2 TB butter

• 1 TB avocado oil

• 1/4 cup chopped fresh Italian parsley

• Salt and pepper as needed

Directions

1. Preheat the oven to 450 degrees Fahrenheit and adjust the oven rack to the middle shelf.

2. Place the lardons in a cold 10-inch Dutch oven or casserole pan. Place over medium heat, cooking until the bacon has rendered its fat and the bacon is browned. Using a slotted spoon, transfer the bacon to a small plate and set aside.

3. Blot the beef with paper towels, ensuring it is very dry, or it will steam in the pan and not brown. Reheat the bacon fat until it is almost smoking, and place some of the beef in the pan, ensuring space between each piece to allow it to brown properly. Do not overcrowd the pan. You may need to do this in 2-3 batches, removing each browned piece of beef with a slotted spoon and adding it to the reserved cooked bacon on the plate.

4. In the same bacon fat, lightly brown the carrot and onions. Pour out any excess fat from the pan.

5. Return the beef and bacon to the Dutch oven with the vegetables, season with salt and pepper, then sprinkle on the flour, tossing the pan contents to coat it evenly in the flour.

6. Set the casserole in the hot oven and cook for 4-5 minutes. Carefully remove the casserole from the oven, toss the beef mixture around, and return to the oven for 4-5 minutes more.

7. Remove the casserole from the oven and lower the heat to 325 degrees.

8. Move the beef to the outside edge of the casserole, leaving an empty space in the center. Add the tomato paste and garlic, stirring with a wooden spoon.

9. Pour in the wine and enough stock or broth so the meat is just barely covered. Add the thyme and bay leaf. Bring to a simmer on the stovetop, cover with a lid, and transfer to the lower third of the 325-degree oven.

10. While the beef is cooking, prepare the pearl onions. Heat a skillet, add the 1-1/2 TB avocado oil and 1-1/2 TB unsalted butter. When the mixture begins to bubble, add the peeled pearl onions and

sauté over medium heat until the onions begin to brown, rolling the onions around to brown all sides. When the onions have browned, pour in 1/2 cup of the stock or broth and simmer until tender. Set aside.

11. Heat the 1 TB avocado oil and 2 TB butter in a skillet until the mixture begins to bubble. Add the mushrooms and sauté until they have lightly browned. Season with salt and pepper and reserve.

12. When the meat is tender, pour the contents of the casserole into a sieve set over a saucepan. Wash out the casserole and return the beef-bacon mixture to it. Add the cooked pearl onions and mushrooms.

13. Skim the fat off the sauce in the saucepan. You should have 2 1/2- 3 cups of sauce. If it is too thick, use filtered water or mild stock to thin it. Taste for seasoning.

14. Pour the sauce over the meat and vegetables in the Dutch oven. Bring to a simmer over medium heat and cook for 5 minutes more, stirring and basting the meat as necessary. The stew can be eaten immediately or cooled and refrigerated to serve the next day. If serving the next day, remove from the fridge 30 minutes before serving. Place the casserole over medium heat, bring to a boil, then down to a lazy simmer for 10 minutes.

15. Serve over buttered egg noodles, boiled potatoes, or rice. Garnish with the chopped parsley, and enjoy!

Chapter 4
Newport, RI

My time aboard Synchronicity opened the door to a string of offshore deliveries. Before long, I was sailing back and forth between South Florida and the Caribbean like it was a commute. I was learning the ropes of the sailing industry while sharpening my cooking skills. My crewmates, bless them, became my unsuspecting guinea pigs.

During that stretch, I made Fort Lauderdale my temporary home base. I lived in transient crew housing, my entire life stuffed into a single oversized North Face backpack. Between deliveries, I picked up work as a day laborer—polishing, sanding, cleaning, painting—whatever kept me close to the docks. Yachts always need attention, and captains love cheap, motivated help.

When winter wound down, most vessels headed north to the Northeast or across the Atlantic to the Med. I was still green—plenty of miles under my belt, but less than a year of real industry experience. The idea of trading open water for concrete wasn't appealing, so I set my sights on New England's sailing mecca: Newport, Rhode Island.

Before they launched their program at Chelsea Piers, my old friends, the Scarano brothers, had run a similar operation out of Newport. I called Rick and told him straight—I didn't want to manage anything, just sail. He was happy to have me back in any capacity. I tied up loose ends in Lauderdale and hitched a ride north.

Newport remains one of my favorite places on earth. The city is steeped in sailing history, with weathered stone buildings, cobblestone streets, and a harbor that feels like a living postcard. Crime is virtually nonexistent, unless you count open-container citations and the occasional public urination—both courtesy of the local sailors.

Since I wasn't managing Adirondack, only sailing her, the pay was modest. To keep my bank account afloat, I picked up a job waiting tables at a new steakhouse opening on Bowen's Wharf. I joined the launch team as part of the opening front-of-house staff.

That experience was an education in itself. The chefs and managers were absolute food and wine nerds—in the best possible way. I was merging my two passions, sailing and food, but keeping enough distance between them to avoid burnout. I barely knew anything about wine, so when our manager, Shawn Westhoven, suggested I read Windows on the World Complete Wine Course, I dove in. Before long, I was a marginally educated wine snob with an opinion on tannins.

That summer, an effortlessly cool woman joined Adirondack's part-time crew—Amy Coleman, host of the PBS show Home Cooking with Amy Coleman. I'd never seen her show, but plenty of our passengers had, asking for autographs and pictures on nearly every sail.

Amy had burned out on the grind of kitchens and food TV. She'd come to Newport to decompress—to do something fun with no pressure. She'd also been an instructor at the Culinary Institute of America, the very place I secretly dreamed of attending. Since I had more schooner experience than she did, we made an even trade: I taught her the ropes of sailing, and she became my culinary mentor.

That summer, I shared an apartment with two of my steakhouse coworkers, Aaron and Suzanne. When I wasn't sailing, serving, or out at the bars, I was cooking for fun—usually testing recipes on

Amy, who critiqued every dish with precision and kindness. She drilled technique into me—how to treat ingredients with respect, how to coax flavor through patience. I'd eaten artichokes all my life but never knew how to properly cook them until Amy taught me. I was terrified of lobster until she walked me through it.

Before that summer, I'd never had real access to professionals in food and wine. This was before the internet overflowed with tutorials and influencer chefs. If you wanted to learn, you read books—or found a mentor. I got both.

I'm sure Shawn and Amy eventually grew weary of my relentless questions, but they never showed it. They encouraged me to keep going, to follow the spark. Looking back, they planted the first seeds of my culinary career. Everyone who taught me afterward was simply watering what they'd already sown.

Lobster Salad with Minted Lime and Coconut Sauce

Yield: 4 servings

This lobster salad has become my go-to for al fresco lunches. You can cook the lobster yourself, or something I do when I work in homes with poor ventilation and very expensive decor. I have the fishmonger do it for me. You can also skip the lobster altogether and substitute crab or cooked shrimp. This dressing is really great on anything, though. It doesn't have to be shellfish. Try it with cooked, shredded chicken, pulled pork, or leftover grilled anything!

Ingredients

For the sauce

- 1 abundant cup of fresh mint (not peppermint)
- 6 oz unsweetened coconut milk
- ½ cup fresh cilantro
- 1 scallion
- 1 tsp honey or maple syrup
- 1 whole jalapeño (1 Serrano or 2 jalapeños with seeds if you like it spicy)
- ¼ cup fresh lime juice
- ¼ cup extra virgin olive oil
- 1 tsp Fleur de Sel

For the salad

- 3 1-¼ - 1-½ pound cooked lobsters
- 1 TB Agrumato lemon oil
- 10 oz cleaned salad greens of choice
- Fleur de sel, as needed
- Fresh lime juice, as needed

Garnish

• Fresh lime wedges

• Picked cilantro leaves

• Picked mint leaves (torn into smaller pieces if the leaves are large)

Directions

1. Place all of the sauce ingredients in a blender. Purée until smooth, season to taste, and refrigerate until ready to use.

2. Cut the lobster into desired size pieces. Place in a glass bowl and mix with the sauce. Taste for seasoning and adjust as necessary. Set aside while you prepare the salad greens.

3. Place the salad greens in a large bowl. Drizzle over the lemon oil and mix the salad to coat each salad leaf. Season with salt, and mix again. Add some fresh lime juice to taste.

4. Divide the salad greens among four plates. Top each salad with the lobster salad. Garnish with lime wedges, cilantro, and mint leaves. Serve and enjoy.

Chapter 5
September 2001
My first and only stinkpot

Part I — The Stinkpot

The Newport season was drawing to a close, and it was time to make winter plans.

I was dating Dave, a young yacht captain, who suggested we apply for a couple's position aboard a 108 'Broward motor yacht scheduled to head south in a few weeks.

I had never worked on a "stinkpot"—the affectionate insult "blowboaters" used for motor yachts. Sailors considered themselves purists, bound to wind and muscle, while power yacht crews ran on fuel and polish. The two tribes respected each other in passing but rarely swapped flags.

I hesitated. Sailing had stripped me down to something simple and pure. No televisions, no satellite phones, no smartphones—just wind, rope, salt, and people. Most nights, we sat on deck under soft amber light, drinking cheap beer and teaching one another knots. The bowline, the clove hitch, the rolling hitch—hours would pass, the sea black and endless around us. It took me three nights to master Tom Fool's Knot, which wasn't much good for sailing but worked wonders for handcuffing a handsome stranger with nothing but rope.

Those were the nights that built me. I never went anywhere without my pocketknife and marlinspike. I was a sailor now—

scrappy, windburned, endlessly curious. The people around me were my tribe: kind, adventurous, unhurried by landlocked concerns.

The motor yacht world, by contrast, seemed sterile. Deckhands with perfect hair and nervous smiles, captains obsessed with polish and protocol. They looked perpetually tense, as if afraid to scuff the reflection of their own boats. But the pay was good—dangerously good.

So, with a mix of curiosity and defiance, I agreed to apply. The yacht needed three positions filled: a first mate, a chef, and a stewardess. Dave went for mate; I went for stewardess, secretly hoping I could work my way into the galley. We interviewed, smiled, and left certain we'd nailed it.

We hadn't.

Days later, after a late restaurant shift, I walked to Dave's apartment. I knocked. And knocked. When he finally opened the door, he looked wrecked—drunk, disheveled, and caught mid-lie.

"You can't come in," he said.

"Is there someone else in there?"

He pursed his lips and nodded slowly.

I turned and walked away before he could see me cry, grateful, through the hurt, that I wouldn't be trapped on one hundred and eight feet of fiberglass with him in the middle of the ocean.

The next morning, I called the captain of the Broward and asked if he'd consider hiring me alone. That's when I learned the real reason we'd been rejected: Dave's forearm tattoos would show under uniform. In the early 2000s, yacht owners could dictate "aesthetic preferences" without consequence. Captain Lance, unfazed by my lack of ink, offered me the job on the spot.

Part II — The First Voyage

We left Newport as the weather turned, the sky silvering over Narragansett Bay. The 108 'Broward gleamed like money—sleek, quiet, obedient to throttle instead of wind. Our passengers were the owner's wife and mother, both named Mrs. Jones. Captain Lance brought in a friend, Nick Cutler, to help crew.

Without a chef, I volunteered to cook, determined to earn my way into the galley. Between meals, I polished chrome, changed sheets, and ran on adrenaline.

Our first stop was Chelsea Piers—my old stomping ground. I rushed through Whole Foods and Balducci's, my arms full of ingredients I hoped would impress. (If I could do it again, I'd start at Union Square Farmers Market, but back then, I didn't know better.)

We left New York on a brilliant September morning. The air smelled like steel and promise. I narrated the harbor as if the Mrs. Joneses were charter guests: the Holland Tunnel ventilators, the classic yachts, the Twin Towers rising ahead like bookends of the sky, the Statue of Liberty turned slightly as if listening. Passing under the Verrazzano, I took one last look back at my city and promised I'd return.

The Jones ladies were gracious and curious, and Nick adored my cooking. He was a lifelong sailor, the kind who could read the wind by the way your hair lifted. I served him a bowl of Thai curry one afternoon in the wheelhouse. He tasted it, paused, and asked for cilantro and lime. When I brought them, he stirred them in, took another bite, and his whole face lit up.

"Mate," he said, "this is bloody brilliant. You should be a chef."

It was the first time anyone had said those words to me.

They landed like an anchor dropped straight into my chest—solid, certain, impossible to ignore.

Part III — The Day the World Changed

The rhythm of life onboard settled into a hum—work, cook, clean, repeat.

Then one morning, that hum cracked.

Lance's phone rang in the galley. His girlfriend was frantic. He turned on the small satellite TV bolted to the wall, and there it was— a plane striking the North Tower. For a few moments, none of us spoke. It didn't seem real. We guessed it had to be an accident— some lost pilot, a tragic one-off.

Seventeen minutes later, the second plane hit. The image burned itself into memory, all sound gone except for the collective intake of breath.

Then came the Pentagon. Then the collapse.

Then silence.

I tried calling my sister. Nothing. She worked in the Financial District and usually commuted from Queens by train. I called again. Again. Finally, a click—and her voice. She'd stayed home that morning. I slid down against the galley counter, shaking with relief.

Outside, the sky was clear. The sea was calm.

But inside the boat, and inside all of us, something fundamental shifted.

For days, we floated in a haze of disbelief and grief. Names began to surface—people I'd known from my hometown, my father's barbershop, the pizzeria where I'd worked in college.

The loss was personal now.

And yet, amid the smoke and sorrow, something else emerged— an unexpected gentleness. As we made our way down the Intracoastal, flags appeared on nearly every dock and porch. In the marinas, strangers nodded, offered coffee, helped with lines. A quiet understanding had taken hold.

A week later, I flew home to New York. The plane banked over Manhattan, and from the window, I saw the city's heart still smoking.

On the streets, people were different—softer, slower to anger, quicker to help. Tragedy had burned away the sharp edges for a while, and beneath them, I found a version of New York I'd never seen.

Part IV — Currents of Chaos

The days that followed 9/11 were heavy with silence. The hum of the yacht's engines felt almost disrespectful, the steady churning of something that shouldn't be moving when the world had stopped.

We made our way south—Savannah, then the Florida line—until a storm forced us to duck into St. Augustine. The sky bruised purple, the air thick with warning.

We secured the Jones ladies on a flight home before the airport shut down and settled into stillness while the storm passed.

The wind howled through the rigging, a sound I usually loved. That week, it sounded human—crying, mourning.

When the eye moved past, I ran into old schooner friends, Psy and Aesa, two pirates in human form. Aesa dragged me to my first hurricane party, where we toasted with Dark 'n Stormies until the windows rattled with laughter instead of wind. When the skies cleared, we untied our lines and slipped south again, chasing calm.

Near Cape Canaveral, the yacht trembled, then went quiet. The kind of silence that only engines can make—total, dreadful, final.

Water in the diesel. Both engines seized. We were a dead thing floating in the Intracoastal.

Captain Lance's face looked hollow under the wheelhouse light as he turned to Nick for captainly advice.

"What would you do, mate?" he asked Nick.

Nick stared out the window for a long beat, the ocean gleaming black beyond.

"Well," he said, deadpan, "with that fifteen-knot northerly, I'd hoist a spinnaker and sail my arse to Lauderdale."

We laughed, and the tension broke. Laughter at sea is oxygen.

Hours later, Sea Tow arrived and dragged us to Melbourne, FL. Nick departed for his home in Mallorca. I hopped a flight to visit my family while engines got repaired. When I returned several days later, the yacht's engines were repaired. We limped south, grateful for motion again.

In Lauderdale, Lance gave me my first shot at being the yacht's cook- a trial dinner. I cooked straight from books, following recipes like gospel, and failed a few dishes in spectacular fashion! Lance didn't scold. He offered training instead. "We can keep you on a stewardess and bring in a chef you can learn from," he said.

The chef they found was freshly minted from culinary school, confident to the point of cruelty. His food was fine; his teaching, nonexistent. Every misstep was my fault, every silence a punishment.

Still, I learned. Not technique—not yet—but something truer: the kind of chef I would never become.

Part V — Storm Lessons

By the time we reached Miami, another storm was brewing. We spent nights trying to secure the yacht against the surging tide, fender boards snapping in the dark.

I suggested adding a third fender, a trick from my sailboat days. The first mate shot me down—"You're interior crew, not deck."

Hours later, a neighboring sailor wandered over, tied a third fender, and the problem disappeared.

The mate apologized. I smiled, salt-stung and exhausted. It wasn't about being right; it was about being heard.

When dawn broke, the storm had passed. We steamed toward Key West under a clean sky, the curse of the broken bowl finally behind us. The Joneses arrived smiling, the new teak deck glowing like honey in the sun. For once, everything gleamed—inside and out.

Part VI — The Vanishing Tender

After Key West came Antigua. We were running tight, the schedule thinner than the fuel filters. Captain Lance hired extra crew, including a new first mate, Mike, and we began towing the 29-foot tender with strict fifteen-minute checks.

On my night watch, I logged the tender under the spotlight, then handed off and fell into my bunk.

An hour later, pounding on my door. Mike's voice, anxious.

"Dana—are you sure the tender was there?"

"Yes. I wrote it in the log." I shouted through the cabin door before opening it to see Mike's nervous face.

"It's gone."

The air left my lungs. We were thirty miles north of Cuba, south of the Bahamas. Lance burst into the wheelhouse with charts and compass, eyes sharp and tired. We traced drift patterns under the glow of red lights, zig-zagging through darkness, scanning the void.

At first light, nothing. Mike hailed the Cuban Coast Guard in Spanish. They'd seen no vessel.

Thirteen hours later, we turned back to course, defeated. The tender—worth a fortune—was gone.

Mr. Jones took the news well; insurance would cover it. Or so we thought.

When Lance returned from his call, his face was gray. The policy excluded towing, night travel, and Cuban waters. We'd been unknowingly violating all of the insurance company's policies.

Moments later, a call came over the VHF in rapid Spanish. Mike translated, his voice flattening: thirty Cubans found dead near a capsized twenty-nine-foot boat, less than a mile from where our tender disappeared.

No one spoke. The engines hummed, and every note of that sound felt like guilt.

We carried that silence for days, the sea stretching around us like a confession we couldn't make.

Part VII — Puerto Plata

When the fuel tanks ran low again, the second batch was contaminated—another cruel echo of before. We flipped back to the cleaner reserve and studied the cruising guide for the nearest port. Puerto Plata, Dominican Republic. The guide warned: avoid unless emergency.

We were living the definition.

From offshore, the coast shimmered, postcard-perfect. Inside the bay, it changed—rickety shacks, stray dogs, men on bicycles selling live chickens from wooden crates. A crowd gathered as we neared the dock, voices overlapping, hands outstretched for our lines.

A man stepped forward, broad and confident, speaking English. He'd arrange clean fuel—for a thousand dollars and tips for every dockhand who touched a rope. Lance paid.

We cleaned down the boat, and for the first time in weeks, I felt sunlight that didn't feel like punishment. A wiry man pedaled up to Mike with cold El Presidentes, insisting he take them. Then Mike disappeared below to help in the engine room.

Hours later, the engines roared back to life—a sound so welcome it bordered on holy. "Let's get out of here before dark," Lance said. We slipped our lines, the crowd cheering and waving us off. Their joy was disarming. For a moment, I wondered if generosity was their only currency.

Part VIII — The Stowaway

St. Thomas greeted us in the small hours, the harbor still and moon-lit. We tied off, ready for quick rest. I volunteered for trash duty.

On my walk back from the dumpsters, I caught something in my periphery—a pair of legs dangling from the flybridge. At first I thought it was crew, but everyone was forward talking to the dockmaster.

The legs moved. My breath froze. I screamed.

A man dropped down from the flybridge, unsteady and wild-eyed. My crew ran toward the noise, forming a wall between us. Security arrived, flashlight beam cutting through the dark. The light hit the man's face, and Mike gasped—it was the same Dominican who'd brought him beer in Puerto Plata.

While we'd been elbows-deep in the engine room, he had climbed aboard, hidden under the green canvas of the dinghy covers, and stayed there—forty-eight hours without food or water.

The security guard, a local man married to a Dominican woman, quietly pleaded with us not to report him. He promised to help the man—clothes, work, shelter.

We agreed.

In the galley, I turned leftovers into sandwiches and wraps, my hands trembling. When I passed the food to him, he tore into it with the hunger of a man who hadn't eaten in days. I watched as something changed in his eyes—a flicker of life returning. Gratitude, raw and wordless, spilling out in the curve of his smile.

That moment branded me.

I grew up in a land of abundance, where "hungry" meant you'd skipped lunch. Feeding him was the first time I'd fed someone who truly needed it. When I hear the word gratitude, I still see his face.

I never learned his name, but whenever I find an El Presidente, I lift it quietly to the memory of our stowaway and hope he found peace.

That night, Captain Lance gathered us on deck. His voice was calm, but the edge of fear lingered underneath. "That's how vessels get taken over," he said. "He could've been anyone, done anything. We got lucky".

He paused, scanning our faces under the low red lights.

"Go to bed. Rest. We leave in two days."

Part IX — The Sky Falling

We spent those two days polishing every inch of the Broward, scrubbing away weeks of chaos. Even the 14-foot inflatable the stowaway had hidden beneath came out immaculate, as if it, too, wanted redemption.

When we finally cast off for Antigua, the sky was clear, the air sweet with diesel and salt. The forecast promised a meteor shower. We left Charlotte Amalie just as the sun sank, the horizon flashing that rare burst of green—a sailor's benediction.

Night unfolded around us, black and endless. Then a streak of light. Another. Then a curtain of stars began to fall.

It was quiet, the engines a low hum beneath the universe unraveling overhead.

I stayed on the flybridge long after my watch, wrapped in salt air and wonder. It felt like the sky itself was shedding its skin, burning the old world away.

Somewhere in that silence, I realized I had to leave.

Not because of the chef or the chaos, but because my instincts had shifted. I felt like a cat on her ninth life—still standing, but running out of grace. Too many close calls. Too many chances borrowed.

By dawn, the meteors faded and Antigua rose out of the horizon like a promise.

We docked, began prepping for the boat show, and I finally told Lance I planned to move on. He took it well, said I'd been a great stewardess but was clearly meant for something else.

Later that day, while I was ironing sheets in the Joneses' stateroom, Mr. Jones came by. He smiled, asked what it would take to make me stay. "Why are you leaving?" he asked.

I paused, looked up from the steam, and said,

"Mr. Jones, I have a college degree, and I'm ironing sheets."

Mr. Jones lowered his head and cracked a smile "well, when you put it like that, I completely understand! We've really enjoyed having you on board with us. If you ever change your mind, there will be a job here for you."

*Farmer's market ingredients ready to grind into chili paste for Thai curry:
shallots, chilies, garlic, lemongrass, fresh ginger and spices.*

Thai Red Chicken Curry
Yield: 4 Servings

Thai curry paste comes in a variety of colors, indicative of the type of chili and blend of spices used in the mix. When local organic chilies and aromatics are abundant, I make my own and freeze it in small batches. Oftentimes, however, I use a good store-bought red or green curry paste, my favorite brand being Maesri. I love the flavor, and it does not contain a bunch of ingredients that cannot be pronounced. This recipe calls for the Maesri brand. If you utilize another brand, keep in mind that it may be more or less spicy.

Ingredients
- 2 pounds Organic Boneless, skinless chicken thighs
- 2 TB Coconut Oil for browning the chicken
- 1 tsp kosher-sized sea salt or to taste
- 2 TB filtered water
- 1 tsp Coconut oil for starting the sauce
- 1 TB Maesri Brand Red Thai Curry Paste
- 2 tsp Thai Fish Sauce
- 1 tsp maple syrup or honey
- 2 cups broth
- 1 kaffir lime leaf, 1" section of lemongrass, or 1 tsp lime zest
- ½ inch slice of fresh ginger
- ¼ cup coconut cream
- 1-½ tsp fresh lime juice
- ½ cup fresh leaves, picked or chopped
- ¼ cup fresh mint leaves, torn
- ¼ cup fresh basil leaves, torn
- 4 lime wedges for garnishing

Directions

1. Dry the chicken thighs very well with a paper towel. Cut the chicken thighs into quarters, and blot them dry again. Reserve on a plate or tray

2. Heat the 2TB coconut oil in a Dutch oven, rondeau, or wide braising pan. Season the quartered chicken thighs with the sea salt. When the oil is hot, but not smoking, add the seasoned chicken thigh quarters and brown on all sides. Do not overcrowd the pan. You may need to do this in more than one batch, depending on the size of your pan.

3. When the chicken has browned, transfer it to a large bowl. Do not wash out the pan. Add the 2TB filtered water to the pan. Using a fish spatula or flat-sided wooden spoon, scrape all of the browned bits from the pan so they mix with the water. Pour the scraped brown bits and water into the bowl with the reserved chicken.

4. Wipe out the pan. Add the remaining 1 tsp coconut oil to the pan. And place over medium heat. Spoon the Thai curry paste into the oil and let it simmer for a few seconds until fragrant. Add the maple syrup or honey, the Thai fish sauce, then add the broth, kaffir lime leaf and slice of ginger. Return the chicken to the pot with the broth and simmer until the chicken is tender, about 15-20 minutes.

5. When the chicken is tender, whisk in the coconut cream and lime juice. Season to taste.

6. To serve, stir in the herbs, ladle into warmed bowls, and serve with lime wedges.

7. This dish is best when served with steamed Jasmine rice (recipe follows).

Steamed Jasmine Rice

Yield: 4 servings

Thai curry is best served over steamed Jasmine rice. I always choose the Lundberg brand. Lundberg brand implements regenerative farming practices. They also test their rice to ensure that arsenic levels are in a safe range for consumption.

Ingredients

- 1 cup Lundberg organic Jasmine rice
- 1 1/2 cup filtered water
- 2 tsp extra virgin coconut oil
- Pinch of salt

Directions

1. Wash the rice: place the rice in a large bowl. Fill the bowl with cool filtered water, and swish the rice around- the water will be cloudy. Drain out the water, leaving the rice in the bowl. Do this several times until the water runs clear, then strain the rice in a fine-meshed sieve and set aside.

2. Add the coconut oil to a pot and place over medium heat. Add the washed rice to the pot and toast in the oil until slightly fragrant, about 30 seconds. Add the filtered water and a pinch of salt. Place a tight-fitting lid on the pot.

3. Bring the mixture to a boil, then immediately turn it down to a very low simmer. Set a kitchen timer for 15 minutes. Allow the rice to cook, undisturbed, on a low simmer.

4. After 15 minutes, keep the lid on the rice and remove it from the heat. Allow the rice to stand in the covered pot for 10 minutes to complete the steaming process.

5. When the rice has completed steaming, fluff it with chopsticks or a fork and serve immediately.

Chapter 6
Johno

The stinkpot was an adventure straight out of an action film—thrilling, chaotic, and not the way I wanted my story to end.

I've sailed close to twenty thousand offshore miles in my life, and that kind of time at sea changes you. It teaches reverence. It teaches humility. Mostly, it teaches that we are all just one short breath away from death. So, I promised myself to steer toward happiness and purpose. I needed to be sailing—and I needed to be cooking.

Captain Lance and Mr. Jones both gave me their blessing to find my next position, so I wasted no time. The Antigua Charter Yacht Show was swarming with opportunity and old friends, so I dove in, determined to find my next boat.

At boat shows, yachties play dual roles: keep the vessel immaculate by day, and turn into charming hosts for the endless stream of charter brokers touring the decks. At night, the marina transforms—flowing champagne, heels clicking on gangways, music rising between the masts. Networking and partying are often one and the same.

I drank like…well, like a sailor back then, so my memories of the night I met Captain John Graham—"Johno," as everyone affectionately called him—are painted in soft focus. There was laughter, a tangle of accents, and a sea of twinkling lights reflected on the water. Someone mentioned that a British captain was looking for a cook. I scribbled the name S/Y Oasis on a napkin.

The next morning, still half-drunk but determined, I dragged myself out of bed at dawn to type up a sample menu and print my CV. My bloodshot eyes hid behind Maui Jims as I made my way to Oasis.

Captain Johno met me at the passerelle, nursing his own hangover. His grin was wide, his honesty refreshing.

"Bloody hell," he said. "That sure was a party last night! I'm feeling it today!"

There was something instantly likable about him— approachable, genuine, steady. Johno reminded me of vanilla ice cream, but not in the plain way people mean it. Vanilla is complex— sweet, earthy, comforting. It goes with everything, and everyone loves it. That was Johno.

He told me about Oasis, his current home: an Ocean 71 that had circumnavigated the globe over five years. He'd started as mate under the previous captain before taking over when his mentor moved on to a larger yacht. He was now rebuilding his crew—a mate and a cook.

As we talked, I learned that Captain Nick Cutler was one of Johno's good friends. Nick had already given me a glowing recommendation. That, combined with Johno's small-crew budget, meant I was a perfect fit.

He offered me the job on the spot.

Since the yacht's next charter season wouldn't begin immediately, Johno suggested I take a few weeks off before joining. "Use the time while you have it," he said. "You'll thank me later."

He was right. I went home to New York, hugged my family, and gathered the last bits of my life on land before heading back to sea.

Two weeks later, I flew into St. Maarten with my life packed into a single suitcase—plus another one full of cookbooks.

Johno met me at the airport and insisted on carrying my bags.

"Bloody hell, what've you got in here? Another human?" he joked as he loaded my cookbook case into the taxi.

We drove to Palapa Marina, where the Oasis tender—a bright red RIB—waited beside the dock. The yacht lived on a mooring in Simpson Bay Lagoon, meaning the dinghy was our daily commute. The cab dropped us off in front of The Soggy Dollar Bar, the unofficial heartbeat of the marina.

Before we shoved off, Johno swept his arm over the little red boat like a game show host revealing a prize.

"This is our car," he announced in his proud British lilt. "We keep her clean and full of fuel. Treat her right and she'll get you home."

Out on the lagoon, the water shimmered green-blue, and Oasis appeared—sleek, white, and poised, tethered gently to her mooring like she was waiting for us.

Johno showed me my quarters below deck: compact, warm, and surprisingly cozy. I unpacked carefully, stowing my knives and arranging my cookbooks while he teased me about how many I'd brought. "You planning to open a library down here?" he said with a wink.

That evening, we went ashore for "sundowners"—sailor code for drinks at the end of the day. In the yachting world, sundowners rarely ended with the sun.

We met a lively crowd of young captains and crew at the Soggy Dollar. They ripped into Johno for hiring "a Yank," and I gave as good as I got. The teasing was affectionate, quick-witted, and relentless. I'd found my tribe again—people who worked hard, played harder, and spoke fluent sarcasm.

We had a few quiet weeks before the first charter, which Johno insisted I use wisely. "Get your dive certification," he said. "Every good cook needs to know how to fetch their own lobster."

So I did.

My qualifying dive was on a sunken shipwreck just off St. Maarten's coast. The moment I descended, the noise of the world vanished, replaced by the sound of my own breath. Sunlight sliced through the surface in long, golden ribbons, illuminating coral like stained glass. Schools of fish moved as one body, shimmering and fluid. The wreck lay before me like a cathedral—silent, ancient, claimed by the sea.

In that stillness, I understood something profound: everything down there—every coral branch, every fin, every fragment of shell—depended on everything else. I surfaced feeling small in the best possible way, drenched not just in salt water but in awe.

Part 2 — The Crew of Three

Johno's good friend Phil, an Aussie with a sun-baked grin and a laugh that promised trouble was never far behind, joined us soon after as our mate. From the first handshake, it felt like we'd known each other for years. The three of us fell into rhythm effortlessly—working, laughing, teasing. It didn't take long before Oasis felt less like a workplace and more like a floating family.

We traded stories, swapped music, and passed books back and forth like currency. I loved learning their slang, their humor, their culture. They loved teaching me.

On evenings off, we'd head to Grand Case, a small beach town on the French side of the island that smelled of butter and ocean. Grand Case was the culinary heartbeat of the Caribbean—every block glowing with candlelight and garlic. There, among the laughter and clinking wine glasses, I tasted dishes I'd only read about in Bourdain's Kitchen Confidential. Those nights became my classroom.

Back on the yacht, I'd try to recreate what I'd tasted—duck confit, bouillabaisse, sauces that terrified me. Johno and Phil ate everything without hesitation, offering equal enthusiasm for triumphs and disasters. Between cooking sessions, I pored over The Professional Chef from cover to cover, dog-earing pages and testing recipes until the galley smelled of my ambition.

Our weekends were sacred—no guests, no uniforms, just us and the sea. We'd spend the day windsurfing or kiteboarding on Galleon Bay until our arms gave out, then drift to Orient Bay for sushi and champagne at Kon Tiki. By sunset, we'd end up at The Sunset Beach Bar, the infamous spot beside the runway at Maho Beach.

Every Sunday, locals and yachties gathered behind the chain-link fence as Air France's flight to Paris revved for takeoff. We'd grip the fence and wait for the engines to roar, laughing like maniacs as the jet blast lifted us off our feet and pelted us with sand and gravel. The first time, I thought it was exhilarating. The second time, I realized it was idiotic. I still went a third.

Part 3 — First Charter, First Lessons

By the time charter season rolled in, we were dialed in and ready. The itinerary read like a sailor's dream—Antigua, St. Kitts and Nevis, St. Barth's, both sides of St. Maarten, the Virgin Islands, and Puerto Rico.

Our rule on charter was simple: I cooked, and Johno and Phil handled the dishes after every meal. It gave me a chance to sit down, breathe, and reset before the next service. My timing in the galley was dreadful, but my food was good, and the guests were patient.

One night, after a week of perfect charters, a guest asked if I could make sushi.

"Of course," I said, with the reckless confidence of someone who absolutely could not.

I had no experience and no idea what I was doing. But I had cookbooks—mountains of them—and I'd eaten enough sushi to fake it. When dinner rolled around, I had everything prepped except the actual rolls. I was standing over a bamboo mat, sweating, sea air thick around me, when Johno leaned through the galley hatch.

"How long till dinner, Chef?" he called down.

My answer must have sounded less than convincing, because seconds later he was beside me, grinning.

"Dana," he said, watching me fumble with a sheet of nori, "you've never made sushi before, have you?"

I bit my lip, shook my head, and braced for a lecture. Instead, Johno washed his hands, tied on an apron, and said, "Step aside. Let your captain handle this one."

He showed me how to roll the first piece—gentle but firm, the rice just right, the seaweed sealed with a thumbprint of water. We fell into rhythm: he rolled, I sliced, Phil delivered. The guests raved, asking for seconds, then thirds. By the end, we'd used every scrap of fish on board.

When we finally cleaned up, Johno looked at me and said, "See? Easy as pie. You'll be showing me next time."

He never scolded, never condescended. Johno taught through laughter.

Over the months that followed, he taught me how to make sashimi from the tuna we caught off the stern, how to clean, scale, gut and filet the local grouper, how to dance on tabletops without spilling a drink, and how to make even the hardest days feel like stories worth retelling. His joy for life was contagious, a kind of quiet magic that pulled everyone into its orbit.

Part 4 — Northbound and Star-Spanked

When the Caribbean season came to a close, Oasis turned north for New England. Before we left, we threw one last wild party with our crew friends from other yachts—music, laughter, and that bittersweet feeling of goodbyes under starlight.

The passage north took over a week. Phil had never been to the States, so I made it my mission to teach him all things American—history, idioms, and, of course, The Star-Spangled Banner.

Johno and Phil were pranksters of the highest order. When my birthday came, they gave me a new gift every hour: matchbooks from our favorite bars, a turtle keychain, a single flip-flop, a British-flag thong that said Mind the Gap. Each one wrapped like a royal present.

By the time we reached the U.S., they had one final act planned. Dressed head-to-toe like caricatured tourists—cargo shorts, fanny packs, sunhats—they broke into a song they'd written themselves:

"Oh say can you see,

From the bollocks of your captain!

What so proudly we drank,

At Antigua's Last Lemming!"

I laughed so hard I cried. Then snorted. Then cried harder.

We'd made it—our first major delivery as a crew. Salt-caked, delirious, and exhausted, we'd found family in one another. Our next season would take us through New England's harbors, where I'd introduce them to my home waters the way they had introduced me to theirs.

Those two men—Johno and Phil—did more than teach me sailing and laughter. They opened doors, introduced me to crews of world-class yachts, and unknowingly set the stage for the next great chapter of my life: cooking for some of the most powerful people in the world.

But before any of that, we were just three sailors chasing wind, sunlight, and a good story.

Grouper is a very popular fish in the Caribbean. One day while free diving for lobster in Tortola, Johno surfaced with a giant grouper in his hands that we prepared simply with mango salsa. You do not have to use grouper. You can substitute almost any fish here, the most important factor being that the fish is fresh. I prefer to cook fish with the skin on, making the skin crispy and edible. If you choose not to serve the fish with the skin, I recommend you cook it with the skin on anyway, as it helps to insulate the fish's delicate flesh from the heat, preventing it from drying out. Be sure to ask your fishmonger to scale the fish (scales are inedible) and pull the pin bones out for you.

The choice of pan is important for crispy skin fish. My preference is a French black steel pan or cast iron skillet. Many choose a nonstick pan for ease of use, but it results in less flavorful, less crispy skin and leaches toxins into the food, depending on the brand. It may take a few tries to master the technique, so remember- even if your fish skin gets stuck, you can still serve it and enjoy it without the skin.

The mango salsa is a recipe open to flexibility. Don't like mangoes? Substitute the mango with any other seasonal fruit. Tomato, summer peach, autumn Bartlett pear, pineapple, papaya…the possibilities are endless. This recipe calls for red onion, but as with most recipes, I use what is local and in season, frequently substituting local scallions, shallots, or even freshly sliced ramps in the spring.

A note on mangoes: The mango tree emits a sap that is frequently found on the outside of the fruit. Many people are allergic to this sap. I always make sure to wash the outside of the fruit very well with soap and water as soon as I get the mangoes into the kitchen. If I know there is a mango sap sensitivity or allergy, despite having washed the fruit, I remove the skin on one cutting board and transfer the skinned fruit to a clean cutting board for dicing to prevent any potential allergic reaction.

You don't have to use grouper for this recipe. You should swap out the fish based on what's seasonally available in your region of the world. Here, the crispy skin technique is applied to porgy, a delightful mild-fleshed sweet fish that is highly abundant on the east end of Long Island.

Crispy Skin Grouper with Mango Salsa

Yield: 4 servings

Ingredients for the fish:

- 4 grouper fillets (6-8 oz each), scaled, skin on, pin bones removed
- Avocado oil, as needed
- Salt, as needed
- 1 garlic clove
- 2 sprigs fresh thyme
- 1 TB pastured unsalted butter
- 4 Fresh lime wedges

Ingredients for the salsa:

- ½ cup red onion, small dice
- Zest of 1 lime
- Juice of 1-2 limes (about 2 TB)
- 2 cups peeled firm-ripe mango, medium dice
- ¼ cup red bell pepper, small dice
- 1 jalapeño, seeded and finely diced
- ¼ cup chopped cilantro, mint, or basil (or a combination of all three!)
- 1 tsp Agrumato blood orange or tangerine oil (extra virgin olive oil can be substituted)
- ½ tsp Fleur de sel

Directions:

1. Prepare the fish: Lay the fish on a work surface, skin side up. Pat the fish dry with reusable or paper towels. Using your chef knife at a gentle angle, gently glide the blade from the tail end to the head

end of each fish filet using your knife blade like a squeegee. You should see moisture collecting on the blade. Wipe the moisture off of your knife with a clean towel, then glide the knife like a squeegee from the head end to the tail end of the fish, removing the moisture from your blade with a towel. Repeat this process multiple times, squeegeeing each filet back and forth until your knife no longer collects moisture. Pat each filet dry one more time with a dry towel and set aside.

2. Prepare the salsa: Place the diced onion in a bowl. Sprinkle with 1/2 tsp of fleur de sel, mix, then add in lime juice and zest. Proceed to prepare the remaining ingredients, add them to the bowl, and mix thoroughly. Add additional seasoning to taste and set aside while you cook the fish.

3. Place a cast iron skillet over medium heat, and add enough avocado oil to cover the bottom of the pan in a thin layer. Brush the fish skin with additional avocado oil and season the flesh side with salt. When the oil begins to shimmer, add the fish filets, skin side down. You can either use your fish spatula or a small pan lid to keep the fish skin pressed to the pan while it cooks.

4. When the fish has cooked about 75% through (you'll see the top is still somewhat raw), remove the pan from the heat. Add the butter, garlic clove, and thyme to the pan. Carefully flip the fish filets over, then using a large spoon, baste the fish skin with the hot, fragrant butter, allowing it to crisp some more.

5. Serve the fish fillets with the mango salsa, and enjoy.

Chapter 7
Sag Harbor

My first visit to Sag Harbor, NY, was on Sailing Yacht Oasis. The yacht was booked for a week-long charter during the July 4th holiday, beginning in New York Harbor.

It was the summer after 9/11. New Yorkers were rebuilding following the most massive tragedy my generation had ever experienced. The fireworks display was slated to be the most magnificent the city had ever seen. A synchronized display, shot off at three different locations around Manhattan on her surrounding rivers. There was so much excitement around the 2002 NYC fireworks. We, as a crew, felt fortunate to experience such an incredible event from the most pristine vantage point…and get paid for it!

While en route to NYC from Newport, RI, aboard S/Y Oasis, the gimbal on my galley stove had broken. The gimbal is a pivoting mechanism that attaches to the stove, allowing cooking surfaces to remain level while the galley to which it belongs is not. When a boat is heeled over, cruising, or bobbing around like a cork in the waves, a yacht chef still needs to cook safely, and the gimbaled stove allows that to happen. It's actually quite a simple, but very cool thing to see in action. Many tragic burns and food losses at sea have been prevented by the gimbal.

The problem required immediate attention to prevent the stove from fully breaking off of the mount and sailing across the yacht's interior. Captain Johno handed the helm over to me while he and our first mate, Phil, descended to the galley. The problem was behind the stove, so Johno rested the whole unit on his shin in order to reach the parts that needed adjustment. The process took a few hours, but Johno fixed the problem and the galley was back in business!

The following day, Johno's leg turned purple and swelled up like a balloon. He became very pale, almost blue, and was clearly in immediate need of medical attention. His then-girlfriend (now wife), Jenni, was living in Manhattan at the time and rushed him to the hospital. As it turns out, the stove resting on his leg for such an extended period of time had cut off circulation, causing Johno to develop a blood infection. He would not be able to captain the charter. While in the hospital, Johno did what any good captain would do. He called Nick Cutler.

Captain Nick happened to be available and flew in to save the week. Based on my previous experience with Captain Nick during the infamous Intracoastal stinkpot voyage, I knew we would be in good hands. Our first mate, Phil, and I felt an immediate sense of relief. Johno would be able to take the necessary time to get well, and Nick would (literally) take the helm like the badass skipper he is!

Since three synchronized fireworks displays were being launched across the city, Captain Nick chose the lower East River—where we could take in all of them at once—as our vantage point. It was perfect. When the first bursts of color lit the skyline, the city erupted in joy. The air vibrated with music, cheers, and the collective heartbeat of a place determined to feel alive again. New Yorkers were celebrating like they never had before—wild, grateful, unstoppable.

We stood on deck, grinning like kids, knowing we'd given our guests an experience they'd never forget. It was one of those nights that burned itself into memory. I'd never felt prouder of my city, or more certain that no matter where the sea carried me, New York would always be home.

The next morning, Oasis pushed off the dock at "sparrow's fart," as Johno used to call it, at first light. We steamed up the East River through Hell's Gate and out onto Long Island Sound. We collected our charter guests at a marina on Long Island's north shore and sailed due east for several hours until we reached Sag Harbor.

Captain Nick docked the boat at the marina just in time for the guests to make the dinner reservation they had scheduled ashore. Nick, Phil, and I tidied up the boat and decided to explore the quaint little village. Long before Sag Harbor was considered a "Hampton," it was a historic whaling village. It is very rich in history with the magical charm that comes along with every New England seaside village. I was smitten and knew in my core that I would one day call Sag Harbor my home.

The gentleman who had chartered Oasis had gifted the last two days of his charter to his personal assistant as a " thank you" to her for all of her hard work. The young lady invited her entire family, who happened to be Chinese. I was told that they would bring all of their own food, and that I would just assist them in the galley.

This jovial Chinese family arrived with cooler after cooler filled with delights I had never previously experienced. The most notable food being the pork ribs made from the family's special recipe, ribs that Captain Nick and I shamelessly devoured when offered to us!

A few short days later, Captain Johno was finally back in good health. He returned to the yacht, relieving Captain Nick of his duties, all of us grateful for Nick's never-ending willingness to help a friend out of a jam. We spent the rest of the summer back and forth from Sag Harbor to Newport, Martha's Vineyard, Nantucket, and Maine.

There were several charter guests that summer who opened some very important doors for me as time went on.

One was a very lovely lady named Olivia. She introduced me as an aspiring young chef to the higher society folks in Millbrook, NY. Later on, this would allow me to pay my way through culinary school at CIA, by cooking weekend dinner parties as a private chef for a handful of clients in the Hudson Valley.

The other was a young couple named Angus and Lily, who decided to purchase a sailing yacht of their own and hired Johno to be the captain. I would eventually work for Angus and Lily in Sag Harbor several years later.

The last major influential yacht charter guest was Annabel, who would eventually hire me to cook in Boston.

The Chinese lacquered pork ribs recipe that follows is one I first learned while studying at the Culinary Institute of America. Chef Cheng taught it in her kitchen, where the scent of ginger, sesame and soy hung in the air like perfume. The moment I tasted the finished ribs, I was transported—straight back to Oasis, to that Chinese family and the night Captain Nick and I devoured their ribs like we hadn't eaten in weeks.

Over time, I made the recipe my own. Adjusted the balance of sweetness, heat, and acid. Learned to coax that deep mahogany glaze to cling just right. Once I felt I'd truly mastered it, I started serving the ribs to my clients. One guest loved them so much she asked for them at the close of every charter. "I want them to be the last thing I eat before I fly home," she told me. A fitting finale—sticky fingers, sweet smoke, and a satisfied grin.

One afternoon in St. Maarten, my captain's good friend Trey came by the yacht after the owners had departed. The plan was simple: hang out, unwind, then hit the town. The captain had told me stories about Trey—a musician, always on the road, promoting his new album. I'd never heard of him, figured he was another guy hustling for a break in the business.

When he arrived, the captain brought him down to the galley for an introduction. I handed Trey a plate of ribs, coconut rice, and Asian vegetable slaw. He looked like he'd had a long night and was more than ready for a real meal. While the captain worked on deck, Trey and I chatted—just small talk and laughter about old New York parties and late-night gigs. He was humble, easy company, the kind of guy who makes you forget the world outside the galley.

Halfway through his plate, I said, "So, Trey, the captain tells me you're quite the budding musician."

He looked up from his ribs, smiled that lazy grin, and said, "Yeah, I guess I do OK."

Later that night, with our bellies full and spirits high, we hit the town together. It wasn't until later that I learned Trey was Trey Anastasio—lead guitarist and co-founder of Phish. So not only does he have great taste in food, but as a musician… I guess he does OK!

Chinese Lacquered Pork Ribs

Yield: 5 racks

Ingredients:

5 racks baby back pork spareribs, cut into 3 rib sections

Painting mixture

- 3 TB Tamari soy sauce
- 3 TB Amontillado (dry) Sherry wine

Marinade

- 2 cups hoisin sauce
- 1 ½ cups unsweetened tomato ketchup
- 2 TB fresh garlic, grated on a rasp grater
- 1 TB minced fresh ginger
- 1 tsp minced jalapeño
- 4 ea Scallions, thinly sliced
- ¼ cup Shao Xing (Rice wine)
- 2 TB toasted sesame oil
- 1 TB kosher-sized sea salt
- ⅓ cup honey

Lacquer coating mixture

- ½ cup honey
- 1 TB toasted sesame oil

Preparation (Day Prior):

1. Place the ribs in a hotel pan large enough to hold all of the ribs.

2. Whisk together the soy sauce and sherry "painting mixture." Brush liberally all over the ribs.

3. Mix together the marinade ingredients and pour over the ribs, being sure to coat evenly. Cover the pan and marinate the ribs in the refrigerator overnight.

Day of Service:

1. Preheat the oven to 325°F. Line 4 half-sheet trays with aluminum foil (this is for easy cleanup later). Place a roasting rack on top of each foil-lined sheet tray.

2. Remove ribs from the marinade and arrange on the roasting racks. Bake for 1 1/2 hours or until ribs are tender.

3. Whisk together the lacquer coating mixture. During the last 20 minutes of cooking, brush the lacquer mixture all over the ribs.

4. When the ribs are ready, remove from the oven and allow to rest for 10 minutes before slicing them into individual ribs.

Chapter 8
From Sea to Land
My First Billionaire Kitchen

Sailing Yacht Oasis was booked for a charter in Southwest Harbor, Maine—home of the famed Hinckley boat builders. Charles and Annabel, the charter hosts, extended an invitation that would change my life: "If you ever want to get off the yachts, come cook for us in Boston."

I'd become obsessed with recreating recipes from the cookbooks I was devouring, longing for a real kitchen instead of a pitching galley. Captain Johno gave me his blessing to go.

Charles and Annabel didn't need a full-time chef, so they flew me to Boston to cook a tasting dinner for their close friends, Carrie and Mike, who were also looking for part-time help. They flew me first class—something I'd never experienced—and set me up with a car service and a suite at The Boston Harbor Hotel. I felt like royalty.

The tasting went beautifully. More than the food, it was the connection that sealed it. Carrie was quirky, sharp, and unfiltered in the best way. She recognized the giant dork in me and matched it. Despite my lack of formal training (I was still reading recipes line by line as I cooked), they offered me the job.

I went back to Oasis, packed my sea bag (and cookbooks!), bought sweaters and a winter coat, and flew home to the Hudson Valley to regroup before heading north.

The next morning, I got a call from the head of Human Resources at Charles's family office to finalize details. At twenty-five, I had no concept of what a family office was. When she explained that her entire company existed solely to manage one family's personal affairs, my mind spun. I'd stepped into a world I didn't know existed.

A background check was required, which came back clear except for a $30 cable bill left over from my college apartment. Then came the NDA—my first taste of the world of confidentiality. The family's chief of security explained it bluntly:

"Dana, you'll be privy to information that might seem harmless to share but could endanger you or our principals. For example, if you tell someone that Charles rides his bike every evening at six, that could create a pattern for someone to exploit. Abduction, ransom—real risks. This is not casual information."

WHOA. That was the moment I realized I'd stepped into a different universe—one I'd only seen in movies.

The Boston Chapter

My repertoire was modest, but I had a few dishes Charles, Annabel, Carrie, and Mike enjoyed. Annabel was a lacto-ovo vegetarian, so I could easily modify the menu—serve everyone the same meal and simply leave the meat off her plate.

Carrie and Mike were a contrast. Carrie was fitness-minded and disciplined—except when sweets were involved. She kept junk food out of the house because she couldn't resist it. Mike was the opposite: a blue-collar guy with a thick Boston accent and a deep love of spice, meat, and beer. They'd met years earlier when he'd done some contracting work on one of her homes—boy meets client, and the rest was history.

They lived just north of Boston and gave me a beautiful apartment above a converted barn on their property. For me, it was paradise. I spent my days cooking, reading, and watching the Food Network, testing new recipes on them each week.

The Brownies and the Burn

One day, Mike challenged me to make the spiciest dish I could. He wanted to test his limits. At the same time, he asked if I'd bake him a batch of brownies while Carrie was away for the day. I decided to do both.

The jerk marinade I made came from my time in the Caribbean—ten Scotch bonnet peppers blended with allspice, ginger, and garlic. I'd once used jalapeños as a substitute back in the States, but this time I wanted the real deal. I even left in the seeds and ribs for maximum heat.

Later that afternoon, when I returned to start dinner, I discovered Carrie was home after all—and the brownies were missing. I tore through every cupboard. She appeared at the kitchen door with a sheepish look.

"Looking for the brownies?" she asked.

I nodded.

"I ate them," she confessed.

"All of them?"

"Yes. My trip got canceled, I came home, and they smelled so good I couldn't resist. I had one, then another, and figured I might as well eat the whole pan so they wouldn't tempt me all week. Now they're gone, and I can move on."

It was a logic I hadn't heard before—but I couldn't argue with it. One day of indulgence, a lifetime of balance.

When Mike came home and discovered the evidence, he was dumbfounded. We all laughed about it. I promised next time I'd bake a secret batch just for him and hide it in his truck.

Then it was time for his spice challenge.

I fired up the grill and carried the marinated chicken out. The moment the meat hit the flames, a cloud of Scotch bonnet smoke hit me square in the face. My eyes burned. I coughed uncontrollably. Mike ran out to check on me, started coughing himself, then grinned through the tears.

"This is gonna be good," he croaked.

Inside, I plated the meal—jerk chicken with mango salsa, sweet potatoes, collard greens, rice, and roasted plantains. Carrie, still in her brownie coma, skipped dinner. Mike sat down like a gladiator facing his final battle.

The first few bites, he smiled triumphantly. Then came the sweat. His voice rasped. "Carrie," he gasped between bites, "I think Dana has won. I can't finish this. I thought I could handle heat, but this… this is another level."

He devoured everything but the chicken, and I learned one of the most important lessons of my early career: just because you can make something hotter doesn't mean you should.

A beautiful bird had died for that meal, and I'd ruined it with ego and ignorance. From that day on, I promised myself to understand spice—to respect its power. If a client wanted heat, I'd serve it on the side, not baked into the flesh of something that deserved better.

Jamaican Jerk Chicken

Yield: 8 servings

When I make this chicken for clients with varying levels of spice tolerance, I will typically make two batches of the spice paste and use habanada peppers in place of the scotch bonnets or habaneros. Habanada chilies have the same flavor and look just like their spicy counterparts but with none of the heat. Habanadas are available at farmer's markets during pepper season and sometimes in specialty markets.

While I typically opt for fresh herbs, this marinade is an exception as it tastes better with dried herbs due to the high acidity level of the marinade.

Ingredients:

• 8 whole chicken legs or 8 chicken breast halves, bone-in, skin on (or 4 of each if you want to serve both light and dark meat)

• Zest of one lime

• ⅓ cup of freshly squeezed lime juice

• 5 Scotch bonnet or habanero chilies, seeds, ribs and stems removed

• 2 TB apple cider vinegar

• 2 TB freshly squeezed orange juice

• 3 scallions, cleaned and coarsely chopped

• 2 TB dried thyme

• 1 TB dried basil

• 1 TB mustard powder

• 2 tsp whole allspice berries, ground

• ½ tsp freshly grated nutmeg

• 1-½ tsp kosher sea salt, fleur de sel, or Celtic sea salt

• 1 tsp freshly ground black pepper

• Lime wedges for serving

Directions:

1. Combine all ingredients except chicken in a blender or food processor. Blend until thoroughly combined. The consistency should be more of a thick paste than a thin marinade. Add a little more orange juice if the mixture becomes too thick to blend.

2. Place chicken in a glass baking dish and brush the paste all over the chicken pieces. Refrigerate for 4-8 hours.

3. Prepare a charcoal grill*. When the coal is very hot, spread the coals to one side of the grill, oil the grill grates, and place the chicken, skin side down, on the cooler side of the grill. Cover the grill and cook for about 20 minutes on the skin side, then flip over and cook for another 15 minutes.

4. Check the internal temperature of the chicken with an instant-read thermometer. When the chicken reaches an internal temperature of 160 degrees Fahrenheit, remove it from the grill and allow it to rest. The chicken will continue carry-over cooking to the 165-degree internal temperature necessary to kill off any potential food-borne pathogens. 5. Serve with fresh lime wedges, and enjoy!

*Jerk chicken is best cooked over charcoal, but can be cooked on a low-gas grill if charcoal is not available. The cooking time will be shorter when cooking over the direct heat of a gas grill, so be sure to use your trusty meat thermometer to know when it's done!

Dark Chocolate Brownies

Yield: one 9 x 13 tray

Ingredients:

- 12 ounces pastured unsalted butter
- 6 ounces finely chopped Valrhona dark chocolate, about 65-85%, depending on preference
- 16 ounces organic granulated sugar
- 2 ounces organic dark brown sugar
- 1-¾ teaspoons (4g) fleur de sel or other kosher-sized grain sea salt
- 6 large eggs, straight from the fridge
- 1/2 ounce vanilla extract
- 1 TB strongly brewed coffee, cooled
- 4-½ ounces organic all-purpose flour
- 4 ounces Valrhona Dutch-process cocoa powder

Directions:

1. Adjust the oven rack to the middle position and preheat to 350°F (180°C). Line a 9-by 13-by 2-inch anodized aluminum baking pan with foil to cover the bottom and long sides of the pan, then cut a piece of parchment paper to fit inside the foil. Grease the non-parchment-lined sides of the pan lightly with unsalted butter.

2. In a 3-quart stainless steel saucier, melt butter over medium-low heat. When it has completely melted, increase heat to medium and simmer, stirring with a wooden spoon or heat-resistant spatula while butter hisses and pops. Continue cooking and stirring, scraping up any brown bits that form inside the pan, until the butter is golden yellow, no longer hissing, and smells like buttered popcorn. Remove from heat and stir in dark chocolate. Allow to rest and cool slightly while making the batter.

3. Batter: Combine granulated sugar, brown sugar, salt, eggs, vanilla, and coffee in the bowl of a stand mixer fitted with the whisk attachment. Whip on medium-high until extremely thick and fluffy, about 6-10 minutes, depending on your mixer's horsepower.

4. Meanwhile, sift together the flour and cocoa powder into a small bowl. When the foamed eggs are fluffy and thick, reduce the speed to low and pour in the warm chocolate-butter mixture. Once it is incorporated, add the cocoa-flour mixture all at once and continue mixing until roughly combined. Finish with a rubber spatula, scraping and folding to ensure the batter is well mixed from the bottom up.

5. Pour into the prepared pan and bake until brownies are glossy and just barely firm, about 30 minutes, or to an internal temperature of 205°F. Cool brownies to room temperature to allow them to set before slicing. Slide a butter knife between the brownies and the edge of the pan, not covered with foil and parchment. Using the foil edges, gently lift to remove the brownies from the pan onto a cutting board. Cut into squares and enjoy. They can be stored in an airtight container for about 5 days at room temperature.

Chapter 9
My Greatest Failure:
How to Lose a Job in Nine Courses…Almost

Several months into cooking for Charles and Annabel, they invited me to accompany them out West for a ski trip. Excited to impress—and inspired by the knowledge that Charles's father was a true foodie—I asked Annabel if I could create a tasting menu one night. She loved the idea and even hired a server to help with the dinner.

Part of my job was to fly out before the family to stock the kitchen and prepare for their arrival. Packing for the trip meant making impossible decisions about what to leave behind. I couldn't bring all of my treasured cookbooks, so I painstakingly copied my favorite recipes by hand. (Ah, the days before the internet.) In the end, I chose three books to bring, two of them by Chef Charlie Trotter. I felt a kinship with him—he, too, had been self-taught—and I was convinced I'd follow his path to culinary stardom. I read his books cover to cover and planned my menu with care. What could go wrong?

Spoiler alert: everything.

The truth was, I had no idea how to work in a professional kitchen. I'd never cooked high-end food for a crowd. My "education" consisted of reading, following directions, and tasting my way through mistakes. Still, I decided to prepare a nine-course tasting menu, complete with Annabel's dessert request: panna cotta. I'd never made—or even tasted—panna cotta in my life, but I had the Charlie Trotter recipe, and that was enough to make me feel invincible.

The night of the dinner began smoothly. The first two courses went out on time and came back with clean plates. I was flying high—until reality hit.

I didn't understand pacing or mise en place. Nothing was prepped, nothing ready to fire. I was still dicing shallots and whisking vinaigrettes as salads were meant to be served. My pasta water wasn't even boiling when it was time for the pasta course. Proteins weren't portioned, the fish wasn't scaled, and the steaks were still fridge-cold.

To make matters worse, I hadn't accounted for altitude—everything cooked differently up there. Every small mistake compounded into a catastrophe. The poor waiter was running interference, returning to the dining room again and again to tell the guests the next course was coming. I don't know how long they waited between plates—hours, probably—but to me, it felt like years.

By the time dessert came, I was ready. I'd made the panna cotta ahead of time, proud of my foresight. Having never tasted the real thing, I sent it out confidently, convinced it would redeem the evening. My triumph was short-lived. When the plates returned, most of the panna cotta was untouched.

After the ski trip, I flew back East with the family—my first time ever on a private jet. I felt like a rock star. Everything I'd dreamed about seemed within reach.

Annabel scheduled a debrief after we landed. She was gracious, starting with the high points. Then came the lows: the steaks were too rare, the pacing disastrous. "We loved the flavors," she said kindly, "but the wait between courses was…long."

I took a deep breath and asked about the panna cotta. I admitted I'd never made—or tasted—one before.

Annabel smiled, a little mischievously. "It was…different," she said. "Panna cotta is usually smooth, creamy, delicate—melts in your mouth. Yours was, well… a bit stiff."

She smirked, and I wanted to crawl under the table.

But instead of firing me, Annabel extended a gift. She'd made a lunch reservation for us at No. 9 Park, an elegant restaurant in Boston's Beacon Hill helmed by one of the few big-name female chefs at the time—Chef Barbara Lynch.

The meal was transformative. I tasted my first piece of perfectly cooked fish, savored braised fennel for the first time, and finally met panna cotta as it was meant to be: soft, quivering, seductive. When the server set it down, it wobbled like the breast of an ample-bosomed woman going for a light jog. The one I'd served, by comparison, had all the bounce and charm of a brand-new implant from an episode of Botched. The difference was night and day—and deeply humbling.

That meal changed me. I realized I needed to taste more and read less. I was lucky to still have a job, and luckier still to have mentors who believed in me. I asked Charles and Annabel for a list of their favorite dishes and restaurants around Boston. On my days off, I explored the city through their eyes—eating, tasting, learning, absorbing.

Soon after, Charles arranged for me to spend time in the corporate kitchen of his father's company. The chefs there took me under their wings, teaching me everything I was willing to learn—which was everything. I'd read The Culinary Institute of America's Professional Chef cover to cover, but this was the first time I'd ever been taught by real chefs. The experience was invaluable.

Just as I began to sense the limits of my self-taught knowledge, Annabel made an incredible offer: she and Charles would pay for me to attend culinary school in Boston if I'd stay on with them.

A dream come true—almost.

Because by then, I knew exactly what I wanted. I wanted the Harvard of culinary schools: The Culinary Institute of America in Hyde Park, New York. I applied, was accepted, and prepared to leave Boston. The decision was bittersweet for all of us, but we knew it was time.

That ski trip disaster became one of the best mistakes of my life.

I'm happy to report that I've since mastered panna cotta—and you can, too. The version that follows is my buttermilk panna cotta: delicate, tangy, and impossibly smooth. It's divine on its own and pairs beautifully with any seasonal fruit—from citrus to Concord grapes.

Spring/ summer: buttermilk panna cotta with strawberry, rhubarb, mint

Winter: buttermilk panna cotta with Cara Cara orange sorbet, candied kumquats and crushed pistachios

Autumn: buttermilk panna cotta & Concord grapes

Buttermilk Panna Cotta

Yield: 6 portions

Ingredients:

- 1-¼ cups heavy cream
- ⅓ cup sugar
- ½ vanilla bean
- 1 ¾ cups buttermilk
- 1TB cold water
- 1 ½ tsp unflavored powdered gelatin
- 1 cup fresh, seasonal fruit, diced

Directions:

1.   Bloom the gelatin: place the cold water in a small prep bowl. Slowly sprinkle or "rain" the gelatin over the water and allow it to bloom for 5-10 minutes.

2.   Place the sugar into a heavy-bottomed 4qt saucepan. Score the vanilla bean lengthwise and open it up to expose the inner vanilla pulp. Using the back of a paring knife, scrape the vanilla pulp and place it in the sugar in the saucepan. Pick up the now scraped vanilla pod and put it in the sugar with the pulp. Stir in the heavy cream, place the saucepan over medium heat, and bring to a simmer, allowing the sugar to dissolve.

3.   Add the bloomed gelatin to the saucepan and whisk lightly. Continue simmering and lightly whisking until the gelatin is completely dissolved. Whisk in the buttermilk and remove from the heat.

4.   Strain the mixture through a chinois or fine-meshed sieve into a large measuring cup or vessel with a spout. Pour the mixture into six 4-ounce ramekins (see note), cover and refrigerate overnight.

5.   When ready to serve, unwrap the panna cotta. Top with diced seasonal fruit and serve.

Notes:

If you want to serve the panna cotta inverted onto a plate, instead of ramekins, use 4 oz aluminum ramekin cups. To invert onto the plate, have a bowl with hot water ready, dip the aluminum cup into the hot water for a second, dry the bottom of the aluminum cup, and invert onto the plate.

Chapter 10
Life at CIA

I applied to the famed Culinary Institute of America in Hyde Park, New York, near the end of my employment with Charles and Annabel. Because CIA's Associate of Occupational Studies program began every three weeks, I used the gap before my start date to pick up freelance yacht cooking jobs with Johno and stash away a little cash.

During that time, I wrote an essay about catching a yellowfin tuna off the aft deck of S/Y Oasis and submitted it for the M.F.K. Fisher Food Writing Scholarship. To my astonishment, CIA awarded me the scholarship—knocking $5,000 off my tuition before I'd even enrolled.

When I moved back home to Washingtonville—about a 45-minute drive from Hyde Park—I decided to commute instead of living on campus. I didn't want to mooch off my parents entirely, so I picked up a part-time job teaching Italian to adults at Mount Saint Mary College. I also cooked private dinner parties in Millbrook, New York.

My introduction to the Millbrook crowd came courtesy of a Hamptons yacht charter guest with a weekend home in the Hudson Valley. When she heard I'd be attending CIA, she practically squealed. The idea of hiring a yacht chef-in-training for her dinner parties thrilled her, and she wasted no time spreading my name around. The pay was exceptional—one Saturday night of private cooking equaled a week's worth of restaurant wages—and it left me time to study and actually sleep.

The first several weeks at CIA were classroom-based: food safety, nutrition, product knowledge. I quickly made friends, sharing stories of my years at sea and my time cooking for billionaires before I even had formal training.

My closest ally was Josh—my culinary soulmate. We were both hopeless food nerds. In between classes, we'd wander the wooded trails surrounding campus, talking endlessly about flavor, technique, and life. When kitchen labs began, we were placed in different classes, which turned out to be a blessing. It meant we could swap stories and compare notes from different instructors.

Josh and I made each other better. He became my right-hand man for private events, and when he wasn't available, I enlisted my friend Jonny Black—now a Michelin-starred chef at Chez Noir in Carmel-by-the-Sea.

Because I'd already devoured The Professional Chef cover to cover—twice—I was well ahead of the learning curve. I became a mentor to many classmates and was elected group leader, earning a small gold pin shaped like a chef's toque. My job was to liaise with instructors before each new course block, gathering intel on what tools and materials we'd need.

Chef Sebald, our German butcher instructor, gave us one of my all-time favorite moments. With his thick accent, he announced that for class we would all need to bring our "six-inch stiff boners." When I repeated the message to the group, I instantly regretted saying it verbatim. At least I didn't refer to the flexible boning knife as "flaccid."

The Climb

The months flew by, and I was tracking to graduate at the top of my class. Paying my own way through school made me relentless.

The harder I worked, the luckier I got. I outworked, outlearned, and ultimately outperformed most of my classmates—earning scholarships, awards, and all-expenses-paid culinary trips, including one to Abruzzo, Italy.

My chef instructors, all impressed by my insatiable curiosity, nominated me for the Food & Wine Classic in Aspen, Colorado. I knew about the event from my yacht days—I'd devoured every issue of Food & Wine and pored over the annual "Best New Chefs" lists. Attending the Classic had been a fantasy of mine, one I never thought I'd realize.

Ten students were invited to Aspen to assist the "Best New Chefs" and "Master Chefs" in cooking demos. None of us knew we'd also be honored as Food & Wine's "Best Student Chefs of 2004," presented by editor Dana Cowin at Aspen's iconic Hotel Jerome. It was surreal.

I was paired with Mat Wolf, a Best New Chef from New Orleans, and my assigned Master Chef was none other than my culinary idol, the legendary Eric Ripert.

Meeting the Master

The event organizers explained that we'd be coordinating through sous chefs and assistants—not the masters themselves. "Under no circumstances," they emphasized, "should you contact your assigned chef directly."

Fifteen minutes after that meeting, my cell phone rang.

"Hello, Dana! This is Eric Ripert."

My jaw dropped. Poker face? Not my skill set.

"Hello, Chef! What an honor—how can I help?"

He wanted to meet in person—with his sous chef, Eric Gestel—to discuss the weekend's prep over cocktails. My CIA instructor,

Chef Andreini, kindly walked me to the restaurant and calmed my nerves along the way.

Ripert sat outside at a picnic table, cigar in hand, relaxed and radiant. He and Andreini greeted each other warmly before my instructor introduced me and slipped away. Ripert ordered me a drink, and we spent the next hour talking about menus, ingredients, and the upcoming demos. When our work wrapped up, he ordered dessert—something special made by a friend of his in the kitchen.

It was exquisite: the tiniest, ripest raspberries resting on clouds of whipped cream between delicate pastry layers. We clinked forks and dug in. The first bite was pure heaven—sweet, creamy, slightly herbal. I couldn't identify the flavor.

"So, what do you think?" Ripert asked.

"It's incredible," I said. "But there's an herb in here I can't place. Tarragon? Basil? Something else?"

Ripert grinned. "Aaah! You know this herb! Let's have another bite and figure it out together."

We did. The herb was cannabis.

Apparently, before legalization, a few daring Colorado chefs had been experimenting with marijuana-infused desserts. And that night, Eric Ripert, his sous chef, and I were their unsuspecting test subjects.

High Times in Aspen

Just as the realization hit me—and the high began to kick in—my phone rang again.

It was Natalie, my fellow CIA student and Aspen roommate. "Oh my God, Dana. I'm so sorry to call, but I'm locked out of the condo."

I covered the receiver. "Chef, would it be okay if she stopped by for my keys?"

Ripert laughed. "Of course! Tell her to come! Bring friends! We are here to have fun tonight!"

Minutes later, Natalie arrived with a few of our fellow "Best Student Chefs." Ripert ordered drinks for everyone, and we sat under the stars for hours, listening to him philosophize about food.

"When you cook," he said, his French accent thick and playful, "you must become the ingredient. Take the carrot! To cook a carrot, you must be the carrot. You must think: I am sweet, I am crunchy, I am… ORAAANNNGE!"

The group roared with laughter.

Back in my college days, I'd been a world-class stoner—my sorority nickname was "Herb." But I'd long since quit. Between the altitude, my lack of tolerance, and the mystery dessert, I was completely gone. Everything from that night blurs together, but I remember one thing: it was pure joy.

The Afterglow

Despite altitude sickness, a raging hangover, and the lingering fog of THC, we were all up early the next morning, ready to work. The festival was a whirlwind of culinary legends: Jacques Pépin, Daniel Boulud, Mario Batali, Wolfgang Puck, Nobu Matsuhisa, Bobby Flay, Alton Brown, Todd English, Scott Conant, Danny Meyer, Drew Nieporent, Ted Allen—it was a veritable hall of fame.

I was overwhelmed with gratitude. For the weekend. For the moment. For the decision to pay my own way through CIA rather than let someone else bankroll my dreams.

My goals had been simple: become a sponge. Learn everything. Master the fundamentals. Fabricate fish. Break down a cow. Bake well enough to respect the pastry chefs. Keep my grades up and earn scholarships.

And I did.

I graduated in the summer of 2005—first in my class.

Chapter 11
Gramercy Tavern
Into the Fire

I am forever indebted to the world of hospitality, the world that taught me the beauty of serving others well. Many people aspire to be waited on, but I'm not one of them. Few things give me greater joy than enhancing someone else's experience with my energy, skill, and spirit.

I've also never been great at sitting still. I'm a doer—my mind and body rarely rest. All of that made Gramercy Tavern the perfect fit for my CIA externship.

At the Culinary Institute of America, an externship is a semester-long immersion in the real world—a chance to put theory into practice and see if you can survive outside the safety net of the classroom.

Gramercy Tavern had been one of New York's finest restaurants since Danny Meyer and Chef Tom Colicchio opened it in 1994. Revered for impeccable farm-to-table cooking and flawless yet unfussy service, Gramercy wasn't just a restaurant—it was a benchmark for true hospitality.

The Best Trial Advice

Competition for externship spots at Gramercy Tavern was fierce. Students from every culinary school applied, but few were accepted—and those who were often worked for free. As an older student with bills to pay, that wasn't an option for me. Luckily, I had top grades, glowing recommendations, and a secret weapon: Chef Corky Clark.

Chef Clark was the master of all things fish. A former Navy man, he ran his CIA kitchen like a military operation. His voice still echoes in my head:

"Clean, dry fish, clean, dry board. Clean, dry fish, clean, dry board!"

When storing fish: "Skin to skin, flesh to flesh. Skin to skin, flesh to flesh!"

Sometimes he'd stop mid-demo and launch into a passionate monologue about how every major war in history was fought over cod. He was one of a kind.

Before I staged at Gramercy, he gave me advice I'll never forget:

"Dana, remember—you're interviewing them just as much as they're interviewing you. Be observant. Listen. Say 'Oui, Chef! ' and do everything with a smile. They may not let you touch food, but if they do—take the opportunity. Show them what you can do without arrogance. And when service ends, you stay. I don't care if you miss the last train home. You stay, help clean, and don't leave until the job is done."

The night before my trail, I barely slept. I sharpened every knife, calibrated my thermometer, reread every mother sauce, pressed my whites, and shined my clogs.

When I entered the staff door of Gramercy Tavern, I had no idea what to expect. A quick tour through the prep kitchens, walk-ins, and pastry area led me upstairs to the main kitchen.

What I saw was pure controlled chaos. The pace was unlike anything I'd ever experienced—like watching a high-speed ballet. The expediter barked tickets in rapid-fire rhythm, line cooks shouting "Oui!" in response, knives flashing under the lights, herbs sizzling in butter, oven doors clanging open and shut. The entire scene was like a culinary version of STOMP on Broadway.

When service finally ended, I made a beeline for every station and asked how I could help break down. A few cooks looked shocked but handed me blue painter's tape, a Sharpie, and items to wrap and label. I scrubbed, swept, mopped—whatever needed doing.

When the kitchen gleamed, one of the cooks handed me a beer. "Right on, chick," he said. "Thanks for the help."

I'm not a beer drinker, but I savored every drop of that one. I'd earned it—and the job.

Thank you, Chef Clark.

Into the Fire

My externship began that spring. I was commuting from a tiny apartment over a bar in Hawthorne, New Jersey. On day one, Executive Chef Johnny Schaefer introduced me to Sous Chefs Nick Martschenko and Josh Cross. I'd be reporting to Josh, who oversaw the Tavern kitchen—a wood-burning grill fueled by Long Island white oak.

Josh hadn't gone to culinary school; his education came from kitchens like Alain Ducasse and Esca. He'd worked under Mario Batali, whose Babbo cookbook I practically knew by heart. Josh was the low man on the sous-chef totem pole, but he worked like a machine.

I learned the hierarchy fast: I reported to Josh, Josh to Nick, Nick to John, and John to Tom Colicchio—long before Top Chef made him a household name.

At first, I worked in the basement prep kitchen. Other externs told me not to expect much more than that—most spent months prepping, rarely glimpsing the upstairs line. But I kept my head down and moved fast.

One day, one of the Argentine prep ladies called me over, her words a blur of Spanglish and hand gestures. I braced myself for bad news. Instead, she smiled and motioned to a new station—with a rubber floor mat. My first Gramercy promotion.

The next morning, Josh came downstairs. "Okay, Minuta," he said. "You've proven you can prep. Time to learn how to cook in a restaurant. Pack up your tools. Meet me at the pass."

Earning My Fire

The upstairs kitchen was different—focused, silent but alive. No music except on Fridays, when Nick Anderer (who'd go on to run Maialino and Marta) controlled the CD player.

Soon I was juggling prep for multiple stations, skipping family meal to keep up. Then, one afternoon, the Tavern roast cook was promoted, the garnish cook moved to roast, and just like that—I became the new garnish-and-sauté girl on the wood grill.

Josh taught me how to build the fire. He took enormous pride in his method and watched me until he was sure I could do it alone. To this day, every time I light a grill, I think of him.

As weeks passed, I began to move with the rhythm of the team. It was intoxicating.

Gramercy was part of Union Square Hospitality Group—then a small family that included Union Square Café, Eleven Madison Park, Blue Smoke, Tabla, and the original Shake Shack in Madison Square Park. Danny Meyer himself would lead monthly new-hire meetings in the private dining room.

There are no words to describe Danny Meyer's energy. As he spoke about his philosophy of "Enlightened Hospitality," I believed my $8-an-hour externship was the best job on earth.

Nick the Badass

The longer I worked, the more Nick Martschenko began to take me under his wing. Nick showed me the kind of chef I wanted to become—and could be—if I devoted myself entirely to the craft.

As Executive Sous Chef at Gramercy Tavern, Nick was a force. A CIA grad and a walking encyclopedia of technique, he could find a faster, cleaner, smarter way to do just about anything. His direction came not as orders but as razor-sharp sarcasm—funny, pointed, impossible to misinterpret. And if you did mess up? That man could move. When things went sideways, Nick was the one who stepped in, fixed it, and restored order before most of us even registered what had gone wrong.

For Nick, it was always about the ingredients. He didn't care whose toes he stepped on if it meant saving a piece of fish or a cut of meat. Each one represented a life—something sacred—and he refused to let carelessness waste it. He'd jump in, save the dish, and then circle back after service to explain the lesson.

In short, Nick was a badass. When he walked through the kitchen during prep, you could feel the atmosphere shift—instant focus, instant respect. He carried authority lightly, with humor and ease. If you were about to screw something up, he'd let you know with a line of dry wit that hit harder than any yell.

With me, though, he was different. Instead of barking, he'd ask questions—what I was doing, why I was doing it—forcing me to think like a chef, not a robot. He didn't just teach me how to cook. He taught me how to understand cooking.

The Breakdown

A few days after I'd been promoted to the roast station, the kitchen was slammed. Tickets were flying in faster than the printer could spit them out, but I was locked in—focused, flowing, completely in the zone. Every protein was fired on time, pans were hot, the board was clean. I was proud of myself. I was owning it.

Then, out of nowhere, Josh appeared beside the grill with another cook from the main kitchen.

"Minuta," he said, "why don't you take a break and go prep downstairs—we've got it from here."

I froze. A break? Now? I wanted to argue, but in a kitchen like that, you don't question the sous chef. You just say, "Oui, Chef," and move.

So I did. I packed up my knives, walked downstairs, and headed straight into the walk-in—furious, humiliated, heart pounding. I had no idea what I'd done wrong. I'd been hitting every mark, and he'd just... benched me.

The cold air hit my face, and I let out a sound somewhere between a sigh and a scream. I may or may not have cursed at a few Lexans of mise en place. Then the door creaked open.

Nick walked in. Of course he did. He grabbed a tray from a shelf, then looked at me.

"Why are you down here?" he asked.

That was all it took. The tears came hot and fast, like a busted dam. I tried to explain through sobs, words tripping over themselves.

"I don't understand what happened! I was crushing it—everything was ready, I was ahead, and Josh just... kicked me off my station!"

Nick set the tray down and crossed his arms. "Yeah," he said quietly, "I saw. You were fine. You were more than fine. But it's your second day, and Josh got nervous. It happens."

He waited for me to breathe, then added, "Next time, you stand your ground. You had it handled. You've earned your station. Don't let anyone take that from you."

I laughed through the tears and made him promise not to tell anyone I'd cried in front of him.

He smirked. "Your secret's safe, Minuta. Now dry your eyes and get back to work."

We hugged it out, I dried my eyes and we walked out together. Service wasn't over yet—and neither was I.

The Potatoes

A few weeks later, in the middle of morning prep, pain shot through my abdomen. I'd had ovarian cysts before, and I knew the feeling. I told Josh quietly that if I disappeared, he'd know why.

Minutes later, as I was checking the Yukon Golds for the potato purée, I barely made it to the locker room before collapsing.

I woke to Argentina waving smelling salts and Scott, the assistant manager, standing over me in his perfectly tailored suit. "The ambulance is on the way," he said.

As they strapped me onto the stretcher and wheeled me toward the elevator, I suddenly remembered. "Scott! The potatoes! They'll burn! Someone needs to get them off the fire or the purée will be ruined!"

He laughed. "Don't worry, Dana. The potatoes are handled. You just get better."

The Exit

I extended my time at Gramercy beyond my externship, staying on to learn as much as possible. The kitchen had become my family—I was even offered a full-time job.. Nick insisted I go back and finish CIA, though, and he was right.

On my last day, I was disappointed to see Nick's name missing from the schedule. I wanted one final service together. But toward the end of lunch, there he was—approaching from the guest side in street clothes.

He'd come in as a diner, just so I could cook for him.

It was the greatest compliment of my early career. That small gesture—quiet, thoughtful, and full of respect—was the perfect ending to my time at Gramercy Tavern. I'll cherish it forever.

Potato Puree Recipe

Serves 4-6 as a side dish

If you do not have a chinois (a cone-shaped fine sieve), you can skip step number 4. The potatoes will not be as refined, but nevertheless delicious!

Ingredients:

• 1 ½ pounds Yukon Gold potatoes, peeled and quartered (about 5 large potatoes)

• 2 TB Kosher-sized sea salt, as needed

• 6 oz heavy cream

• 6 oz whole milk

• 5 oz cold unsalted butter, cut into cubes

• Fleur de sel to finish

• Freshly ground pepper to finish

Directions:

1.   Place the potatoes in a large pot or pan. Add enough filtered cool water to cover by 1 to 2 inches. Season with the salt and bring to a boil. Reduce the heat to low and simmer until the potatoes are tender for about 30 minutes. Drain the potatoes and return them to the pot. Place the pot over low heat, shaking frequently, until any remaining moisture evaporates, about 1 minute.* Heat the milk and cream in a small saucepan and keep warm while you work with the potatoes.

2.   When cool enough to handle, pass the potatoes and the cold butter through a potato ricer or food mill into a clean pot. Add the milk and cream mixture. Stir or carefully whisk until the mixture is well combined.

3.   Pass the potato puree through a chinois into a clean, warm pan.

4.　Season to taste with fleur de sel and freshly milled pepper. Serve hot.

*the texture will be creamier and looser than a typical mashed potato. This purée can also be made a day ahead and reheated, but you may need to add more butter, milk, and cream.

XVOO Mashed Potatoes made with pink-fleshed heirloom potatoes

XVOO Mashed Potatoes

Yield: 4-6 servings

A beautiful alternative to traditional mashed potatoes for the dairy intolerant: extra virgin olive oil mashed potatoes. It is important to use a good quality extra virgin olive oil with a flavor you find pleasing.

Ingredients:

- 2 ½ pounds Yukon Gold or other waxy potato
- 6 whole cloves of freshly peeled garlic
- 1 sprig fresh thyme
- 1 TB kosher sea salt
- 6 oz extra virgin olive oil
- 1 ½ cups cooking water from the potatoes, reserved right before straining the cooked potatoes
- 1 TB extra virgin olive oil for garnishing
- 2 TB sliced fresh chives for garnishing

Directions:

1. Peel the potatoes and cut into 1-2 inch chunks. Place in a large saucepan with the peeled garlic cloves and thyme sprig. Cover the potatoes with cool water by 2 inches (9.0 pH if using Kangen water), and add the salt.

2. Place the pot on high heat. When the water comes to a boil, lower the heat to a simmer and cover the pot with a lid. Simmer until potatoes are tender.

3. Strain the potatoes into a colander, and set over a bowl to reserve the cooking liquid.

4. Pass the hot potatoes through a food mill or potato ricer.

5. Stir in the extra virgin olive oil, then a cup of the reserved cooking water. Taste the potatoes for seasoning. If a thinner consistency is desired, add the reserved half cup of cooking water.

6. Serve in a warm bowl with the TB of extra virgin olive oil and sliced chives as a garnish.

Chapter 12
Bentley, Side Door, 30 Minutes

I'd been working as a yacht chef and private chef for several years. My résumé was rock solid: a CIA valedictorian, six months at Gramercy Tavern, and glowing letters from billionaire employers, yacht captains, and clients. I was highly qualified for almost any private chef position. The only question was whether I still wanted to be one.

I'd just quit a traveling private chef job with an eccentric employer named Stevie—for one reason only: to protect my reputation.

When I started working for Stevie, I was still new to private households and naïvely mistook kindness for friendship. Stevie confided in me constantly, especially after one of the frequent blowouts with staff. Every few months, someone quit—or was fired—and each time Stevie claimed the same thing: the person had been stealing.

After every "theft," Stevie would hand me a list of vendors and tell me to call and cancel the fired employee's credit cards. It made me feel trusted—part of the inner circle. But soon, Stevie's stories started to unravel. Timelines didn't add up. Details shifted. I finally realized I was being manipulated. The "thieves" were scapegoats. And once I knew that truth, I knew my time was coming.

I wanted to believe I was different—that my loyalty mattered—but deep down, I knew better. I'd seen Stevie destroy reputations with a single phone call. In this world, even a whisper of a false accusation can end a career. I began walking on eggshells, quietly plotting my exit.

Since the world wasn't yet fully digital, I armed myself with an accounting calculator and spent days reconciling every expense down to the penny. I inventoried every piece of kitchen equipment, photographed everything, and drafted a resignation letter that gave ample notice.

When I handed Stevie my letter, it was dismissed on the spot. "No need for a transition. You can leave now." Just like all the others.

Two weeks later, the phone rang. Stevie was screaming. The target this time was a CSA membership I'd purchased from a local farm.

"Three hundred dollars without approval?!" Stevie bellowed.

I reminded her that I'd always been told to clear expenses only over $2,000. I explained what a CSA was—Community Supported Agriculture—how the $300 share gave us weekly boxes of produce and a 10% discount at the farmstand. We'd saved over two grand that season thanks to it.

But logic didn't matter. Stevie's fury drowned it out. Finally, to protect myself, I snapped:

"If you disagree, I'll just write you a check!"

She went silent for a moment, then said, "Fine. Mail it."

And that's how I, a working-class chef, ended up writing a check to a multimillionaire for the food they'd eaten. The math was infuriating—Stevie had saved $2,500 thanks to that $300 CSA—but being right wouldn't protect me from lies. My reputation was worth more than the money.

As Sonny says in A Bronx Tale: "It costs you twenty dollars to get rid of him. You got off cheap." For $300, I got rid of Stevie—and considered it a bargain.

Dana Food Begins

The experience left me shaken. I'd worked for incredible, grounded people up to that point, but Stevie made me wonder: What if this is what comes with money? What if everyone at this level is crazy, and I'm the sane one?

Still, I loved the work too much to quit. I loved the hunt—farm to farm, fishmonger to butcher, assembling meals from ingredients that had names, faces, and stories. I loved knowing my clients' dollars were going straight into the hands of small farmers and honest craftspeople. And yes—the paycheck didn't hurt. Private chefs earn about double what restaurant chefs do, sometimes more.

I decided to keep going—but smarter this time. I wanted clients who valued real food and respected the land it came from. People who could taste the difference between a Caesar salad made from lettuce pulled from the soil that morning and one made from shrink-wrapped hearts that had been on a truck for two weeks.

Since my past jobs had come through word of mouth, I decided to enlist the help of a domestic staffing agency. In those days, the private service industry was still small, and getting registered with the top New York agencies was an ordeal. But I did it—every interview, every background check. Then, I waited.

While waiting for the right placement, I filled in for other private chefs during their vacations and kept my knives sharp. I also kept studying, cooking, reading.

One day, while flipping through Edible East End, I found a feature on a new restaurant in Southold, Long Island: The North Fork Table & Inn. It was owned by NYC chefs Gerry Hayden and Claudia Fleming—a culinary power couple. Gerry was known for his work at Aureole and The River Café. Claudia, a James Beard Award winner and the author of my favorite dessert book, The Last Course, had once helmed the pastry kitchen at Gramercy Tavern.

By the time I'd arrived there for my externship, Claudia had already moved on, but her presence lingered. The pastry team still used sheet pans marked with red Xs, her way of warning the line cooks to keep their warped trays off her racks. The legend was that if Claudia found her trays on the line, she'd dump the contents in the trash right in front of everyone and march the tray back to pastry. No one ever tested her twice.

When I read that Claudia and Gerry were opening a farm-to-table restaurant on the North Fork, I knew I wanted in. I drove to Southold, résumé in hand, and asked to stage. They welcomed me immediately.

Working there reignited everything I loved about cooking. Every day began with breaking down Long Island ducks while Van Morrison played in the background. Gerry would show me the day's farm haul—crates of sun-warm tomatoes, just-dug carrots, tiny greens—and we'd talk about how to build the menu around them. The energy was infectious.

For the first time in a long time, I thought about leaving private service behind. But I wasn't quite ready to give up the pay. So, I promised to help at The North Fork Table whenever I could—until the right private chef job came along.

Enter Mr. Stout

Several weeks later, one of the agencies called. A client named Mr. Stout was seeking a full-time chef for his Hamptons estate.

Mr. Stout had built his fortune through brilliance and grit. He lived the kind of life you see in movies like Meet Joe Black—complete with a helicopter commute from Manhattan to the Hamptons every Thursday, returning on Monday mornings.

He adored his Bentley convertible. I'd know, because I'd hear it over the kitchen intercom:

"Bentley, side door, thirty minutes," he'd announce.

Within seconds, George, the assistant butler, was downstairs with a chamois and polishing rag.

Despite the wealth and the staff of fourteen, the Stouts were gracious people who treated everyone with respect. They'd slowed down on entertaining but insisted their team eat well. Every day at noon, I prepared a family meal for the staff—grounds crew, butlers, housekeepers, even contractors. The Stouts often joined us, helping themselves to a plate from the buffet.

I made sure that buffet was a celebration of the Hamptons—fish from the docks, vegetables from nearby farms, cheeses and meats from local artisans. For me, it was heaven.

The abundance reminded me of a revelation I'd had years earlier while cooking in Maine. I'd wandered into a tiny farm market and tasted a Sungold tomato so sweet it stopped me in my tracks. Cilantro so aromatic it perfumed the whole shop. From that day forward, I realized great food didn't need complication—just good knife work, a little salt, and olive oil.

The Hamptons had that same magic. I stumbled upon The Green Thumb Organic Farm in Water Mill one day while lost, and the smell of cilantro there took me straight back to Maine. The women who ran the farm became my friends, and before long I was sourcing nearly everything locally: produce from Green Thumb and Open Minded Organics, cheeses and oils from Cavaniola's, meat from the local butcher, and fish from a nearby monger.

Cooking that way felt alive. It fed me as much as it fed the Stouts and my coworkers.

Dana Food

Mrs. Stout would often wander into the kitchen mid-prep.

"I don't know what it is about your food," she'd say, "but it's just so good."

I'd smile and credit my farmers.

When Mr. Stout wasn't teasing me about portion sizes, he was praising the freshness of his vegetables. Under my watch, he started eating cleaner, craving fewer processed foods. I'd converted a die-hard bar food guy into a farm-to-table fan. He began losing weight in a healthy way without even realizing it.

One afternoon, Mr. Stout called me into the library.

"Dana," he said, "it's an election year. We're hosting a political fundraiser. Normally, we hire Daniel Boulud's team—but this time, we want you to do it."

I froze. Feeding a hundred guests at $10,000 a plate? This was the kind of gig I'd once said would mean I'd "made it." And now, here it was.

Nervous but honored, I immediately recruited Jamie Wagner, a trusted former colleague from Gramercy Tavern—skilled, composed, and unflappable under pressure.

My first menu draft was loaded with luxury: caviar, foie gras, truffles. But when Mrs. Stout reviewed it, she smiled gently.

"Dana," she said, "these guests eat like that all the time. I want them to have good food. Real food. What you make. I want them to taste what we eat."

She listed her favorites: my Caesar salad, the lamb chops, that strawberry sorbet she loved.

Her enthusiasm was infectious. That day, I finally realized how deeply she and Mr. Stout appreciated what I did.

I revised the menu to reflect exactly that—simple, seasonal, soulful. When I handed it to her, she grinned ear to ear.

"Yes," she said. "This is Dana Food."

From that day forward, my style had a name.

A Final Meal

The fundraiser was a huge success. Guests raved, the Stouts beamed, and Mr. Stout proudly introduced me as "our chef" to the presidential candidate running for office.

After that, cooking for the Stouts felt like cooking for family. Sundays became pub-food days—buffalo wings, sliders, crab cakes—his guilty pleasures. Mrs. Stout, instead, enjoyed platters of crudités with fresh dips, steamed vegetables with "a little butter" and her favorite watercress soup. During football season, they were both happy as kids!

That last Sunday, I served him a spread fit for a Super Bowl: pigs in blankets, fried seafood, all the works. He was delighted.

The following weekend, he flew to Palm Beach. I had the weekend off and flew to Ohio to meet my newborn nephew. While waiting on my layover in Philadelphia, my phone rang.

It was Edgar, the estate manager. His voice was quiet.

"Dana," he said. "Mr. Stout passed away in his sleep."

I froze in the middle of the airport, joy and grief colliding in my chest—the birth of my godson and the loss of my favorite boss at almost the same moment. Then I broke down.

A stranger saw me crying and walked up, wrapping me in a wordless hug. Her kindness undid me completely.

That was the day I decided I would dedicate my craft to healthful food. Mr. Stout had been a kind, generous man, loved by everyone who knew him. His passing wasn't just the loss of a great employer—it was a turning point in my life.

At his funeral, I sat with my fellow staff, holding hands as we mourned the man who treated us like family. And I silently promised him this:

I would cook in a way that honored life—never taking it, or its nourishment, for granted again.

Tuna Salad (Mr. Stout's Favorite!)

Yield: 6 servings

Ingredients

• Four 6-7 ounce glass jars of tuna packed in olive oil

• 1 small red onion, minced

• 3 TB fresh lemon juice

• 1 stalk of fresh celery, minced

• 2 medium-sized carrots, peeled and minced

• 1/4 cup extra virgin olive oil

• 1 TB Agrumato lemon extra virgin olive oil

• ¾ cup seed oil-free mayonnaise or homemade aioli

• ¼ cup chopped flat-leaf parsley

• Sea salt to taste

• Freshly ground black pepper to taste

Directions

1. Place the red onion in a large glass bowl. Add the lemon juice, season with a pinch of salt, and allow to sit for 15 minutes.

2. Add the tuna to the bowl and mash it with a fork. Add the remaining ingredients, mix, and season to taste.

3. Serve as a sandwich, with crackers, or enjoy on a bed of lettuce.

Mrs. Stout's Watercress Soup

Yield: 4 servings

This vibrant green soup became a favorite among my high-profile clients for its slimming, detoxifying effect ahead of red carpet appearances. Watercress is rich in antioxidants, iron, and vitamin C, supporting clear skin and a flat stomach while still offering a sense of nourishment.

Served as a light yet satisfying lunch, this soup laid the foundation for a three-day pre-event meal plan, followed by a clean dinner of lean protein (such as grass-fed beef, fish or chicken) and steamed seasonal vegetables.

I prefer to make this soup with water so the flavor of the watercress stands out. You can also use vegetable stock or a nice chicken bone broth if you're looking for more body and want to add protein to the soup.

Ingredients

- 1 TB extra virgin olive oil
- 2 leeks, washed and sliced
- ½ tsp sea salt
- 2 sprigs of thyme
- 1 bay leaf
- 8 oz Yukon Gold potato, peeled and sliced
- 2 oz blanched Marcona almonds
- 16 oz filtered water, vegetable stock, or chicken stock
- 4 oz fresh watercress
- Pinch of nutmeg
- ½ tsp fresh lemon juice
- Additional sea salt and fresh black pepper to taste
- Watercress microgreens to garnish

Directions

1.   Add the olive oil to a 4qt saucepan. Place over low heat, add the leeks, 1/2 tsp sea salt, thyme, and bay leaf. Stir gently with a wooden spoon, cover the pan with a lid, and allow the leeks to sweat over low heat until soft, about 10 minutes.

2.   Add the potatoes, almonds, and water, stock, or broth. Bring the mixture to a simmer and cook until the potatoes are very tender.

3.   Add the watercress, then immediately transfer the soup to a blender or food processor. Pulse, then blend until smooth.

4.   Return the soup to a clean pan. Add the nutmeg, lemon juice, salt and pepper to taste.

5.   Ladle the soup into four warmed bowls. Garnish with the watercress microgreens and serve.

Chapter 13
Ranch Life

All of the billionaires I've cooked for have been avid collectors of real estate. Reed was no exception. He'd just purchased a sprawling ranch out West and hired an elite East Coast architecture firm to design his dream retreat. I was given the honor of feeding Reed and his design team for the first time on the property—christening the brand-new kitchen with its inaugural meal.

I'd been warned the nearest grocery store was forty minutes away, so I planned like a general before battle. I had the ranch managers stock basic staples, then filled a few coolers in New York with specialty ingredients for those first meals. At the FBO—the private terminal that catered to jets like Reed's Bombardier Global 5000—I handed the coolers off to the pilots, who loaded them with the same care one might give crown jewels. Moments later, we were airborne, heading toward the Rockies for the unveiling.

The ranch was breathtaking. A sea of mountains, red dirt roads, and wide-open skies. Rivers and streams snaked through the valleys, stocked with trout. Herds of elk roamed the pastures, wildflowers painted the fields, and cowboys moved cattle through the dust. It was the kind of place that made you whisper when you arrived—because anything louder might offend the silence.

Inside the main house, the design team unveiled a kitchen worthy of Architectural Digest. My excitement curdled into dread when I learned that the only available work surface was a

Nakashima—a $90,000 live-edge slab of wood freshly varnished by the legendary George Nakashima himself. I stared at the glistening surface like it was a museum piece, not a countertop.

I covered every inch with towels, stacking cutting boards on top like defensive armor, transforming the showpiece kitchen into a traveling gypsy setup. My nerves were on high alert, but the meals went off without a hitch—and the Nakashima survived me.

Much of what I served came straight from the land itself: grass-fed beef raised right there on the ranch. At the time, "grass-fed" was a whisper on the wind—something you found at a farmers 'market, not a grocery store. I'd done my homework, reading Joel Salatin's $alad Bar Beef and learning that grass-fed cattle were a different animal entirely—leaner, richer in Omega-3s, prone to drying out if cooked like grain-fed steak.

The flavor surprised me. It was deeper, almost gamey, with a faint metallic edge when overexposed to heat. I learned that high-temp searing—the usual American approach—robbed it of its delicacy.

Sous vide cooking was gaining traction then, and while it promised precision, the plastic barrier between food and heat never sat right with me. BPA-free or not, I couldn't shake the idea of cooking inside a cocoon of chemicals. I wanted purity—fire, salt, metal, and muscle.

That's when I fell in love with the reverse sear. It became my go-to for grass-fed beef and game alike: marinate overnight (or not), cook low and slow in the oven until the interior reached the perfect temperature, then finish with a quick, blistering sear in a pan or over charcoal. It gave me the tenderness of sous vide without the compromise—and the crust of a steakhouse dream.

When I had the chance, I'd finish the reverse sear over a ceramic lump charcoal grill—the kind of grill that breathes like a living thing. The smoke from the hardwood mingled with the beef's natural sweetness, giving it a flavor that could only be described as primal luxury.

During those summer visits, I'd pair the beef with cherry tomato salad and Olathe sweet corn—a Colorado legend. You could always spot the real stuff at the markets: the tops of the ears were trimmed, the worms already cut away. The locals knew the truth—the sweetest corn always came with a few hitchhikers. The farmers had to lop off the tops before the worms made it to the cob. The imperfect corn was always the most divine.

Reed's favorite finishing touch was a drizzle of fifty-year-old balsamic vinegar—not the cheap, caramel-colored syrup from a squeeze bottle, but the kind that had seen half a century of patience. Thick, glossy, almost spiritual in aroma.

Aceto Balsamico Tradizionale di Modena DOP is a thing of devotion. Made from the must of Modena grapes, reduced slowly over open flame, aged in a series of wooden barrels—oak, chestnut, mulberry, ash, and juniper—each lending its own whisper of flavor. It's a liquid chronicle of time itself, evaporating a little each year into the ether—the "angel's share." By the time it's bottled, only a few concentrated ounces remain.

I used it sparingly, like perfume—just enough to let the acidity kiss the meat. Reed would close his eyes, savor the bite, and murmur, "That's the good stuff."

Standing there in that pristine, million-dollar kitchen, surrounded by the smell of woodsmoke, sweet corn, and seared beef, I felt the quiet irony of it all. Here I was, a working-class kid from Washingtonville, cooking on a table worth more than most people's homes, feeding a man who could buy a mountain—and yet, what connected us was something ancient and simple: the primal comfort of good food cooked with care.

That's the real currency of my trade. Not the paychecks, not the private jets. It's the moment someone takes a bite and remembers they're human.

Reflection

Cooking in that stone-and-timber cathedral of a kitchen taught me something I hadn't learned in any classroom or galley. True luxury isn't the marble counters or the price tag on the vinegar—it's the intimacy of a meal prepared with intention. Out there, surrounded by mountains and silence, I realized that food has the power to bridge entire worlds: the billionaire and the ranch hand, the Nakashima countertop and the dirt under a farmer's nails. In the end, the same rule always applies—respect the ingredients, honor the craft, and feed people like it matters. Because it always does.

Reverse-Seared NY Strip Steaks

Yield: 4 steaks

Ingredients:

• 4 NY Strip Steaks, at least 1-½" thick

• Avocado oil, beef tallow, or clarified butter as needed

• Kosher-sized salt as needed

• 1 TB whole butter

Steak marinade ingredients:

• ¼ cup extra virgin olive oil

• 1-½ tsp balsamic vinegar

• 1 clove garlic, minced or grated on a zester

• 1 tsp minced sage leaves

• ½ tsp minced thyme leaves

• ½ tsp minced rosemary leaves

• ½ tsp kosher-sized salt

• Pinch of dried red chili flakes

Directions:

1. Measure all ingredients into a small bowl. Whisk together well.

2. Pat steaks dry with a paper towel. Place in a glass baking dish large enough to hold all steaks in a single layer.

3. Pour the marinade over the steaks. Flip and turn the steaks to evenly distribute the marinade. Cover and marinate for 4-12 hours in the refrigerator.

4. Preheat the oven to 275°F. Place a wire rack on a rimmed baking sheet.

5. Remove the steaks from the marinade, gently wiping off excess marinade. Season both sides of the steak generously with kosher-sized salt and arrange the steaks on the wire rack.

6. Place the steaks in the oven and cook to the desired temperature (follow the chart below). This can take as little as 20 minutes for a rare steak or more than 45 minutes for a medium-well steak. Time will vary based on many factors, so begin checking the internal temperature after 15 minutes.

7. When the steak has reached the desired internal temperature, remove the tray from the oven.

8. Heat a cast-iron skillet large enough to hold all the steaks on the stovetop. If your pan is not large enough to fit all four steaks without overcrowding the pan, use two pans or cook the steaks in batches.

9. Coat the bottom of the pan with avocado oil, beef tallow, or clarified butter. When the fat is very hot and shimmering, gently lay the steaks into the hot oil. You should hear them sizzle. Add the butter and baste the steaks with the hot fat, 45 seconds to a minute on each side. Using a set of tongs, turn the steak onto the thin, fatty side getting a nice crust on the fat.

10. Remove the steaks from the heat and rest on a wire rack for 2-3 minutes and serve. Reverse-seared steaks do not require much resting time.

Desired Doneness	Remove from oven	Target finished internal temperature	Approximate time in oven
Rare	110°F	120-125°F	25 minutes
Medium-Rare	120°F	130-135°F	30 minutes
Medium	125°F	140-145°F	35 minutes
Medium-Well	130°F	150-155°F	40 minutes
Well	145°F	160-165°F	45 minutes

Steak Marinade

Yield: enough to marinade 4 steaks

This marinade is great for any grilled meat, chicken, or fish. If you use it for fish, cut down the marinating time to 1 hour.

Ingredients

- ¼ cup XVOO
- 1- ½ tsp balsamic vinegar
- 1 clove garlic, minced or grated on a zester
- 1 tsp minced sage leaves
- ½ tsp minced thyme leaves
- ½ tsp minced rosemary leaves
- ½ tsp kosher-sized salt
- Pinch of dried red chili flakes

Directions

1. Measure all ingredients into a small bowl. Whisk together well.

2. Pat steaks dry with a paper towel. Place in a glass baking dish large enough to hold all steaks in a single layer.

3. Pour the marinade over the steaks. Flip and turn the steaks to evenly distribute the marinade. Cover and marinate for 4-12 hours in the refrigerator.

Corn and Tomato Salad
Yield: serves 4-6
Ingredients:
- 4 ears fresh corn in the husk
- 1 pint cherry tomatoes
- 2 scallions, thinly sliced
- 1 jalapeño pepper, seeded and minced
- ½ tsp kosher-sized salt
- 1 tsp balsamic vinegar
- 1 TB extra virgin olive oil
- 6 large fresh basil leaves

Directions:
1.   Preheat the oven to 450°F.
2.   Place the corn in its husk on a sheet tray, place in the middle rack of the preheated oven, and cook for 15 minutes, flipping the corn over halfway through. Remove from the oven.
3.   While the corn is cooking, place the scallions in a large bowl. Add the balsamic vinegar and XVOO, then the jalapeño. Cut the cherry tomatoes in half and add to the bowl with the scallions. Gently mix the ingredients around, then sprinkle the salt over top and set aside.
4.   When the corn is cool enough to handle, shuck the corn, removing all of the stringy pieces of corn silk.
5.   Using a sharp chef's knife, slice the kernels off the corn cob and add to the bowl with the tomatoes.
6.   Chop the basil with a very sharp knife or tear it into small pieces with your hands, add to the salad, and mix.
7.   Adjust the salad for seasoning as desired and serve.

Chapter 14
Palm Beach

I had a great aunt who lived in Riviera Beach, Florida, just north of Palm Beach. In 1986, my parents loaded my brother, sister, and me into our brand-new Cadillac Brougham and made the long drive south from New York to spend a week with Auntie Ruth in her beachside condo.

Auntie Ruth was considered wealthy by most standards, though her version of luxury was simple and sun-soaked. We'd spend our days building sandcastles, jumping waves, and hunting for seashells to fill my mother's red glass vase back home. The air always smelled of salt and orange blossom. In the mornings, we'd walk barefoot to the beach, grab a sack of oranges, and twist our "orange squeeters" — those goofy plastic juicers that let us sip juice straight from the fruit. It was the purest form of indulgence I'd ever known: sunshine, sweet oranges, and sea spray.

To my child's mind, that was how rich people lived. Fresh crab claws, ocean air, the sound of flip-flops on concrete.

Palm Beach, I would later learn, was a whole different planet.

By the time I returned as a private chef in 2008, the world had just imploded — the financial crash, the Bernie Madoff scandal — but you'd never have known it standing under the banyan trees on Ocean Boulevard. Palm Beach was untouched. Money doesn't disappear there; it just changes yachts.

The parking lot at Publix told the story. Bentleys, Rolls Royces, Maybachs, and Aston Martins lined up like showroom cars. Some days, when I was forced to parallel park between two million-dollar vehicles, I offered a quiet thank-you to the universe that my employers 'car wasn't the size of my parents 'old Cadillac Brougham.

My clients 'Palm Beach vacations bore no resemblance to the lazy beach days of my childhood. Every minute of every day was accounted for — tennis lessons, golf lessons, cycling sessions, riding in Wellington, private Pilates, charity luncheons, dinner parties. It was a well-oiled, million-dollar routine disguised as leisure. Everyone who had an oceanfront home in the Hamptons seemed to have a mirror image of it here. They'd fly down on their jets every Thursday, fly back Sunday night. Same friends. Same schedule. Different backdrop.

For me, those trips were a blur of constant cooking. I became an architect of sustenance — an engineer of "healthy fuel." Smoothies, salads, pressed juices, protein bars, muffins. So many muffins. The clients and their friends practically lived on them. They wanted food that could move as fast as they did — something they could grab between a tennis lesson and a board meeting.

That's where my Bran Muffins came in. They were humble little things, unassuming next to the gilded kitchens and designer dinnerware. But those muffins were the heartbeat of every Palm Beach trip. I'd make hundreds of them, batch after batch — their scent of molasses and vanilla filling the massive kitchens as sunlight poured through walls of glass.

They became a ritual. I'd line them up on silver trays after breakfast service, each one perfectly domed and gently steaming. The housekeepers would wrap them in linen for the guests to take to the courts or the stables. By midmorning, the trays would be bare.

The muffins were simple, portable joy — the one thing that seemed to slow everyone down for five minutes.

When a guest requested a gluten-free version, I took it as a challenge and got to work. The first batch collapsed like deflated soufflés. The second came out dense as hockey pucks. But by the third round, I nailed it — golden, tender, and just sweet enough. Soon, the gluten-free muffins were as famous as the original. I'd spot them tucked into beach bags, gym totes, even inside the console of someone's Bentley.

Those muffins fueled the billionaires. And in a funny way, they fueled me, too. They were proof that something humble — something born from whole grains, honey, and care — could still be the most coveted thing in a world of excess.

When I did get a rare hour to myself, I'd wander through the quiet Palm Beach neighborhoods, the same ones that once seemed so unattainable. I'd pause to smell the purple bougainvillea, the same kind that lined Auntie Ruth's condo all those years ago. And for a brief moment, the worlds of then and now would overlap — the barefoot kid with orange juice dripping down her chin and the private chef balancing a silver tray of muffins in a billionaire's mansion.

Both of us, in our own way, were just chasing sunlight and sweetness.

Bran Muffins

Yield: 24 standard-sized muffins

These muffins are famous among a handful of very powerful people. I baked them multiple times a week for three years straight because my health-conscious client loved sharing them with friends. They became a staple in the household — everyone ate them daily. I even made a version studded with chocolate chips and shredded coconut for the kids. They're quick, wholesome, and packed with enough fuel to power an entire family's day. And yes… they'll keep everything else moving right on schedule if you know what I mean ;)

Dry ingredients

- 8 oz oat bran
- 6-½ oz whole wheat flour
- 2 tsp (12g) baking soda
- 1 tsp (6g) baking powder
- ½ (4g) tsp salt
- 2 tsp cinnamon
- 1 tsp cardamom
- 1 tsp ginger
- 1 tsp turmeric

Wet ingredients

- 2 eggs
- 5 oz whole milk
- 5-½ oz plain unsweetened yogurt or kefir
- 3 oz extra virgin olive oil
- 7 oz honey (be sure honey is runny and not solid or creamed)
- 1/½ tsp vanilla extract
- Additional ingredients
- 2 oz grated carrots
- 1 very ripe banana, pear or peach, mashed
- 2 oz coarsely chopped walnuts, pecans or almonds

- 2 oz flaxseeds
- 6 oz dried cherries, raisins, goji berries, or cranberries OR 10 oz fresh or frozen berries (if using frozen, do not defrost) extra flax seeds to sprinkle over muffins

Directions

1. Preheat the oven to 375 degrees. Grease 24 regular-sized muffin cups or line them with unbleached disposable liners.

2. In a very large bowl, whisk together dry ingredients. In a smaller bowl, whisk together wet ingredients until very thoroughly combined and emulsified. Pour the wet ingredients into the bowl with the dry ingredients and mix together. Fold in the remaining ingredients.

3. Use an ice cream scoop or large spoon to fill the prepared muffin cups 2/3 full. Sprinkle flax seeds over the top of each muffin. Bake for 20-25 minutes until the muffins are firm, yet springy to the touch. Allow to cool in tins for 15-20 minutes, then invert onto a cooling rack to cool thoroughly.

4. Store muffins in an airtight container for up to two days on the counter, and up to one week in the refrigerator.

5. If making large batches, you may freeze the unbaked muffins in the prepared tins. When baking, do not defrost. Simply take the pan from the freezer and place it in the preheated oven. Bake for 25-30 minutes or until done.

Gluten-Free, Dairy-Free, Refined Sugar-Free Banana Muffins

Yield: 12 muffins

Most people will never guess these muffins are gluten-free if you don't tell them. I love that they do not include arsenic-laden rice flour and various gums that are often required to successfully execute gluten-free baked goods. The most important factor is to ensure your bananas are very ripe with brown speckles, or they will lack the sweetness and pronounced banana flavor one expects of a banana muffin.

Ingredients

- 1 TB coconut oil, melted, plus more for greasing the pan
- 1 TB extra virgin olive oil
- 4 large eggs
- 3 TB honey
- 1 tsp pure vanilla extract
- ½ tsp apple cider vinegar
- ½ cup coconut flour, sifted
- ¼ cup blanched almond flour, sifted
- 1 tsp baking soda
- ½ tsp kosher-sized sea salt
- ½ cup coconut milk
- 3 large bananas, very ripe with brown speckles

Directions

1. Preheat the oven to 350 degrees.

2. Grease the sides and bottom of a standard-sized muffin tin or line with unbleached paper muffin cups. Place the 1TB coconut oil, extra virgin olive oil, eggs, honey, vanilla, and vinegar in a bowl and whisk thoroughly until completely homogenous.

3. Using a clean whisk, whisk together the coconut flour, almond flour, baking soda, and sea salt in a bowl, then add to the wet ingredients, whisking until thoroughly combined.

4. Place the bananas and coconut milk in a separate bowl and mash together until the mixture resembles baby food.

5. Add the banana mixture to the batter and whisk until thoroughly combined.

6. Fill the muffin tins 3/4 full and bake for 20-25 minutes, until a toothpick inserted in the center comes out clean.

7. Remove from the oven and allow to cool in the pan for 10 minutes. Remove muffins from the tin and cool completely on a wire rack.

Dragonfruit Smoothie

Yield: 2 smoothies

This smoothie is cooling and nourishing after a heavy, sweaty, hot weather training session. My clients always crave fruit between tennis matches, but their medical teams suggest consuming fruit with fat and/ or protein to keep glucose levels from spiking. This smoothie achieves that while incorporating a good, clean protein powder to aid in muscle recovery while keeping my clients satiated and energized for their next round of activity!

Ingredients

- ¼ cup raw cashews
- 12 oz coconut water
- 1 TB coconut milk
- ¼ cup frozen mango
- ¼ cup frozen pineapple
- ⅓ cup frozen dragon fruit chunks
- 2 medjool dates, pitted
- 1 tsp grated ginger
- ¼ tsp cardamom
- 1 scoop Truvani unsweetened protein powder

Directions

1. Place cashews, coconut water and coconut milk in a blender and puree until very smooth.

2. Add remaining ingredients, puree until smooth, divide between two glasses, and serve.

Chapter 15
All The Wild Things

I was burnt out in a way only private jet travel can burn you out. To outsiders, it sounded glamorous — flying on sleek aircraft, serving caviar at 40,000 feet, landing in exotic locations — but the truth was far less cinematic. My life had become a blur of flight manifests, shopping lists, and sleepless nights. There was no downtime, no rhythm, just a constant churn between destinations.

While my employers packed their monogrammed luggage and chose spa treatments, I was in a frenzy — sourcing ingredients unavailable in remote corners of the world, updating provisioning lists for estate managers, labeling meals for transit, and packing coolers full of food that had to taste fresh after hours in the sky. By the time we reached altitude, I was elbow-deep in plating trays in a galley the size of a broom closet, assisting the flight attendant in orchestrating meal service while turbulence jostled the Champagne flutes.

When the jet finally touched down, everyone else slept. I planned the next meal. The drive from the FBO to the estate was my only quiet moment — thirty or forty minutes in the backseat of a black SUV, staring out at landscapes that blurred by, already thinking about dinner. The exhaustion ran bone-deep. I used to daydream about sitting in coach on a commercial flight — no menus to print, no silver to polish — just a book in my lap and silence in my ears.

To make things even more complicated, I was doing all of this with my then-husband. The personal dynamic tangled with the professional one, and the weight of our shared burnout eventually cracked the foundation of our marriage. In hindsight, it was inevitable. You can't sustain love when your entire life is service. Couples in the domestic world often don't survive it — too many hours, too much pressure, not enough separation between duty and self.

I thought if I could just find another job — one that gave me space, one that didn't keep us joined at the hip — maybe we'd stand a chance. I sent out word to every contact in the yacht and private staffing circles that I was available for freelance work.

It was Captain Johno who threw me the lifeline. He connected me with our mutual friend June — a former chief stewardess turned global estate manager for a billionaire. June had known me back in my scrappy yacht days, long before culinary school, before Michelin kitchens, before all the "yes chef" and linen uniforms. She remembered the ambitious kid who used to get tipsy on rum punch and talk about one day being a real chef.

Her voice over the phone was electric. "Dana, I've got someone perfect for you. He's sharp, driven, loves great food, and lives on Long Island's Gold Coast. You'll hit it off."

When I arrived at the estate for the tasting, June helped me navigate the maze of construction mud and scaffolding, coolers in tow. Just before we stepped through the service entrance, she turned to me with that mischievous grin of hers.

"Oh — one more thing. I don't think anyone's told you who you're cooking for."

I shook my head.

She leaned in. "Let's just say… he's kind of the Bruce Wayne of billionaires."

She wasn't wrong.

He had the presence of someone born with both power and restraint. Brilliant, athletic, charming, endlessly curious — the kind of man who made you believe the world still rewarded competence and drive. He could talk about carbon sequestration in one breath and surf breaks in Montauk the next. And somehow, after a full day of tennis, polo, and meetings, he still had the energy to play GaGa ball with his kids and their friends until sunset, then head into a private training session.

My first few months were spent as the relief chef, filling in so his full-time chef could take days off. But one afternoon, I got called into a meeting with the director of operations — a man so serious he made accountants look carefree. I braced myself for bad news; in this line of work, a "meeting" often meant a polite goodbye.

Instead, he smiled. "Bruce is… annoyed."

My stomach dropped.

"Annoyed," he continued, "that you're not his full-time chef."

What followed changed my career. Bruce wanted me to oversee his global culinary operations — to train his chefs around the world in my methods, to standardize kitchen systems, and to curate his food program down to the last olive. He wanted REAL ingredients, meals made from scratch in every kitchen. He was offering full creative control — and a salary that made me sit down for a moment to process it.

I accepted without hesitation.

Bruce wasn't just wealthy — he was awake. He understood something most people, even most chefs, didn't: that food is energy, and that the closer you eat to the wild, the more alive you remain.

He hunted his own game, caught his own fish, and filled his freezers not with industrial meat but with animals that had lived on untouched land. He was a man who could afford anything, yet he craved what money couldn't manufacture — the taste of something real.

He preferred everything wild. Venison, elk, wild duck, pheasant, trout, boar — animals that had lived clean lives, untainted by antibiotics, hormones, or confinement. Cooking for him taught me the nuance of wild proteins: how to keep lean meat tender, how to coax depth from the mineral edge of wild flesh, how to honor what came from the land.

In the early years, the game meat arrived butchered the way a hobbyist might do it — uneven, air-pocketed, freezer-burned. I worked with Bruce's gamekeepers and butchers to professionalize the process: vacuum sealing, flash-freezing, labeling with dates and cuts. Within two years, his personal game reserves rivaled the best butchers in Manhattan.

Eventually, Bruce wanted to take things even further — not just wild, but optimized. He brought on longevity specialist Dr. Peter Attia, whose philosophy on health centered around precision nutrition: high protein, low sugar, clean fats, and an obsessive awareness of blood glucose.

That's how I became part of Bruce's health and wellness dream team. Scarlett, his personal trainer, designed the physical regimen. Attia's team provided the data — the macros, the glucose readings, the deficiencies. And I became the architect of his recovery: building menus that restored what his body expended, matching nutrients to training intensity, and designing meals that healed on a cellular level.

Every crumb, every sip, every calorie was logged. Bruce wore a glucose monitor; I tracked his food across time zones. When he dined out, his assistants sent photos of his plates. My phone filled with thousands of food pictures — 60,000 and counting — a visual record of one man's pursuit of peak health.

Bruce's discipline was unwavering. When Attia called for zero sugar, Bruce went cold turkey. He had a sweet tooth when I met him, but once he committed, he never wavered. I've seen billionaires bend every rule in life — except their own when they're truly determined.

When he was sick, I healed him with food. When he traveled, I replaced jet-catered fare with clean, wild ingredients. His private jet galleys carried elk tenderloin and wild-caught salmon instead of foie gras and short ribs. His fuel came from the earth, not the factory.

In time, Bruce Wayne became more than just my employer — he was proof of concept. Proof that nature, when respected and unmanipulated, provides everything we need.

He understood that wild is health. That animals raised on grass instead of grain, fish caught in cold waters instead of pens, produce grown in living soil instead of chemicals — all of it transfers vitality directly to the human body. He knew the future of wellness was not more supplements or more technology, but more nature.

It was my honor to keep that man thriving for over a decade — to feed the mind, the body, and the mission of someone whose work quietly made the world better.

Reflection

Cooking for Bruce Wayne changed how I think about food and life. The wild things — animals, plants, even people — are stronger for having lived without walls. The cleanest energy on this planet comes from what the earth makes without interference. Wild food carries the pulse of the landscape it came from — sunlight, minerals, struggle, and survival.

Bruce knew that before it became a trend. He understood that true health is elemental. That you can't fake vigor; you can only feed it. And that sometimes, the best medicine isn't found in a bottle — it's grazing in a field, swimming in a stream, or flying over the treetops before finding its way to your plate.

Cherry-Dark Chocolate Overnight Oats Recipe

Yield: 1 serving

It is important to utilize organic oats in this recipe so as to not poison yourself with glyphosate, a carcinogenic herbicide used in commercial oat production. Additionally, I always opt for Valrhona dark chocolate as it is one of the very few great-quality dark chocolate brands without elevated levels of lead and cadmium. If you want to avoid oats and grains altogether, you could use chopped nuts in their place. Hazelnuts are particularly delicious here!

Ingredients

- 6 oz organic Greek yogurt
- 1 tsp raw honey
- ¼ vanilla bean
- ½ tsp ground cinnamon
- ½ TB whole flaxseeds
- ½ TB chia seeds
- ¼ cup organic rolled oats
- 1 oz Valrhona dark chocolate, finely chopped
- ½ cup frozen cherries, each cherry cut into quarters

Directions

1. Place the Greek yogurt and honey in a small bowl.

2. Score the vanilla bean lengthwise with a sharp paring knife. Open it up and scrape out the inner vanilla pulp using the back of the paring knife and place the pulp in the bowl with the yogurt and honey. Add the cinnamon and whisk the mixture until all of the ingredients are fully incorporated and homogenous.

3. Stir in the flaxseeds, chia seeds, rolled oats, dark chocolate, and frozen quartered cherries.

4. Spoon the mixture into an 8 oz glass container or mason jar.

Golden Milk

Yield: 2 servings

Golden milk can be made with traditional cow's milk, goat's milk, or any non-dairy milk. For the most nutritional benefit, I often make this with homemade walnut milk. Among nuts, walnuts contain the highest level of Omega-3's. I serve this to clients when they are injured or post-surgery to quell inflammation and boost the immune system.

Ingredients

• 2 cups homemade walnut milk (recipe follows) or other milk of choice

• 1-inch piece of fresh turmeric, peeled and grated, or 2 tsp ground turmeric

• 1-inch piece of fresh ginger, peeled and finely grated

• ½ vanilla bean, scored lengthwise

• 1 tsp ground cinnamon

• ¼ tsp ground cardamom

• 1-2 tsp raw honey (more or less to taste)

Directions

1. Place all ingredients but the honey in a heavy-bottomed saucepan.

2. Place the pan over high heat, bring it to just boiling, then immediately turn the heat to low and allow to simmer for 10-15 minutes.

3. Remove the pan from the heat, and strain the golden milk through a fine-meshed sieve.

4. Sweeten the mixture with the honey, pour into warmed mugs, and serve.

Homemade Walnut Milk

Yield: 4 servings

You can easily make your own non-dairy milk with nuts, filtered water, and a powerful blender. This eliminates the additives, gums, and binders found in most commercially prepared non-dairy milks. I add a touch of coconut cream to give the non-dairy milk a creamier mouth feel, more reminiscent of dairy milk. Be sure to read the ingredient label on the coconut milk to ensure it contains only one ingredient: coconut.

Ingredients

• 1 cup raw organic walnuts

• 3-½ cups filtered water plus additional for soaking

• Pinch of salt

• 2 TB pure coconut cream

Directions

1. Place the walnuts in a 16 oz mason jar. Add enough cool filtered water to cover the nuts by two inches. Place in a refrigerator for at least 4 hours.

2. Drain and rinse the walnuts. Place them in a high-powered blender. Add the 3 1/2 cups of filtered water, the pinch of salt, and the coconut cream.

3. Blend the mixture on high power until it is white, slightly frothy, and very smooth.

4. Strain the mixture through a fine-meshed cone-shaped sieve, pressing it through with a 2 oz ladle. Alternately, strain it through a nut milk bag or a double-layered cheesecloth.

5. Pour the strained milk into a glass jar and refrigerate. Use within four days.

Ginger Immunity Tea

Yield: 6 servings

Whenever I hear one of my clients getting a sniffle or a cough, I immediately whip up a double batch of my ginger immunity tea. This tea is pleasantly assertive. It can also be used to help settle a sour stomach or give a nice jolt of energy to those avoiding caffeine. The tea should be served hot for maximum health benefits, but it can also be served cold or over ice if preferred.

Back when I was in culinary school, one of my buddies, Chef Brendan King, taught me how to peel ginger with a metal spoon. I think of him every time I peel ginger. It's a well-known method, and I think it's just genius. You simply take a metal teaspoon and use the spoon's edge to scrape the outside peel off of the ginger. This allows you to get into all the crevices without cutting your fingers!

Another "ginger trick" I employ is peeling whole ginger knobs and freezing them so they can be easily run over a rasp-style grater. I store the peeled ginger in a pint-sized mason jar and take out the frozen, peeled ginger knobs as needed. It allows me to get a fine grate without all the ginger strings getting stuck in the grater and making a puddle on my cutting board.

If you struggle to find elderberries, you can omit them. This tea is just as delicious without them and still contains very effective healing properties.

Ingredients

- 6 cups/ 48 oz filtered water
- 6 oz whole ginger, peeled and chopped
- 1 TB dried or freeze-dried elderberries
- 3-½ 3 oz honey
- 1-⅕ oz lemon juice

Directions

1. Combine water and ginger, bring to a boil, then simmer for 10 minutes. Turn off the heat, add the elderberries, and allow to steep for 5 minutes.

2. Whisk in the honey and lemon juice until well combined. Strain the tea and serve hot.

Wild Turkey Tonkatsu

Yield: 4-6 servings

Bruce's daughter, Amie, was an incredible shot with a bow and arrow. I always made sure to have ingredients on hand for this family-favorite dish, because any time she set out to procure a wild turkey, we were guaranteed to eat well!

My oil of choice for cooking wild turkey tonkatsu is Hudson Valley Cold Pressed Sunflower Oil. Seed oils have been highly vilified as toxic- and rightfully so. This particular sunflower oil, however, is an exception to the rule. It is cold pressed from raw sunflower seeds in the manner that extra virgin olive oil is made. It is unrefined, contains no solvents or bleaches, and has a smoke point of 374°F. It has a pronounced, nutty flavor. If you cannot find this particular oil, you can use avocado oil. Just be sure to do your research, as some avocado oils are not pure avocado, but a blend of other not-so-good oils.

This recipe calls for only the breast of the turkey. Since I don't believe in cherry-picking certain cuts and throwing the rest of the animal away, I either braise the legs or turn them into sausage. The bones get roasted and boiled down into a turkey bone broth. When an animal gives its life to nourish another soul, it is important to respect the animal's life by letting none of it go to waste.

Ingredients

- One whole wild turkey breast, boneless and skinless
- Organic tamari or soy sauce
- 2 cups organic All Purpose Flour
- 7 whole organic Eggs
- ¼ cup water
- 20 oz (2 packs) organic panko breadcrumbs

- Hudson Valley Cold Pressed Sunflower Oil or Avocado Oil as needed for shallow frying

Sauce Ingredients

- 1 cup organic unsweetened ketchup
- 1-½ ounce good quality oil-packed anchovies
- 3 Tb organic tamari
- 1-½ Tb dijon mustard
- 2 Tb water

Directions

1. Slice turkey breast into 1/2" slices AGAINST THE GRAIN (the most important part of the recipe).

2. Place turkey breast slices in a bowl, season with organic tamari or soy sauce, and allow to marinate for 30 minutes.

3. Place all of the sauce ingredients in a blender and blend until smooth (if you don't have a Vita-Prep/ Vita-Mix blender, you may need to add more water as needed); place in a bowl and set aside.

4. Prepare the 3-stage breading:

Fill a shallow baking or pie pan with the flour. Whisk the eggs and water together in a large bowl. Fill another pan with the panko breadcrumbs.

5. Dredge each slice of turkey through the flour until evenly coated, and shake off the excess. Place the flour-dredged turkey in the egg and flip on both sides until thoroughly coated. Place the egg-coated turkey slice into the tray with the panko breadcrumbs and coat thoroughly. Transfer to a parchment-lined sheet tray and continue this process until all slices have been breaded.

6. Have a clean sheet pan with a rack ready. Pour ½ cup of the sunflower oil into a large sauté pan and heat until the oil just begins to shimmer, not smoking. Working in batches, carefully place each turkey breast in the oil, being careful not to overcrowd the pan.

When each slice is golden brown on the bottom, flip the turkey slice over and allow to cook on the other side until golden brown, then transfer to the rack to drain.* Continue this process until all of the turkey is cooked. Mid-way through, you will need to strain the oil into a clean pan to remove burning breadcrumb pieces and add a bit more oil to the pan.

*If you are uncertain whether your turkey is cooked through, use a digital thermometer. As long as the temperature is 165 or above, it is safe to eat.

To serve: spread a small amount of sauce onto a platter. Cut the cooked turkey into slices, place on top of the sauce, and serve!

Reverse-Seared Elk or Venison

Yield: 4 steaks

When preparing this dish, you want a tender cut of the animal. I do not recommend cooking game meats past medium-rare, but if you like your meat more well-done, this reverse sear method will ensure that your steak is tender and not reminiscent of shoe leather. When grinding the pink peppercorns and juniper berries for the marinade, I recommend using an inexpensive coffee grinder. I always keep one in the spice cabinet that is dedicated to grinding spices and never used for coffee.

Ingredients:

- 4 Elk or Venison steaks
- Avocado oil, beef tallow, or clarified butter as needed
- Kosher-sized salt as needed
- 1 TB whole butter

Marinade ingredients:

- ¼ cup extra virgin olive oil
- 1.5 tsp balsamic vinegar
- 1 clove garlic, minced or grated on a zester
- 1 tsp ground juniper berries
- 1 tsp ground pink peppercorns
- ½ tsp minced thyme leaves
- ½ tsp minced rosemary leaves
- ½ tsp kosher-sized salt

Directions:

1. Measure all marinade ingredients into a small bowl. Whisk together well.

2. Pat steaks dry with a paper towel. Place in a glass baking dish large enough to hold all steaks in a single layer.

3.   Pour the marinade over the steaks. Flip and turn the steaks to evenly distribute the marinade. Cover and marinate for 4-12 hours in the refrigerator.

4.   Preheat the oven to 275°F. Place a wire rack on a rimmed baking sheet.

5.   Remove the steaks from the marinade, gently wiping off excess marinade. Season both sides of the steaks generously with kosher-sized salt and arrange the steaks on the wire rack.

6.   Place the steaks in the oven and cook to the desired temperature (follow the chart below). This can take as little as 20 minutes for a rare steak or more than 45 minutes for a medium-well steak. Time will vary based on many factors, so begin checking the internal temperature after 15 minutes. Game meat is typically best at medium-rare.

7.   When the steaks have reached the desired internal temperature, remove the tray from the oven.

8.   Heat a cast-iron skillet large enough to hold all the steaks on the stovetop. If your pan is not large enough to fit all four steaks without overcrowding the pan, use two pans or cook the steaks in batches.

9.   Coat the bottom of the pan with avocado oil, beef tallow, or clarified butter. When the fat is very hot and shimmering, gently lay the steaks into the hot oil. You should hear them sizzle. Add the butter and baste the steaks with the hot fat, 45 seconds to a minute on each side.

10. Remove the steaks from the heat and rest on a wire rack for 2-3 minutes and serve. Reverse-seared steaks do not require much resting time.

Desired Doneness	Remove from oven	Target finished internal temperature	Approximate time in oven
Rare	110°F	120-125°F	25 minutes
Medium-Rare	120°F	130-135°F	30 minutes
Medium	125°F	140-145°F	35 minutes
Medium-Well	130°F	150-155°F	40 minutes
Well	145°F	160-165°F	45 minutes

Parsnip Puree

Yield: 4 servings

This is a simple, straightforward recipe that can be used for almost any root vegetable, from carrots to beets to celery root. I do not use stock for my vegetable purées. Instead, I use water. This allows the flavor of the vegetable to shine. If you do not want to use butter, you can substitute extra virgin olive oil or a good quality dairy-free butter like Miyokos.

Ingredients
- 1 1/2 pounds fresh parsnips
- 1 TB pasture-raised butter
- 1 sprig fresh thyme
- 2 tsp kosher-sized sea salt
- Filtered water, as needed

Directions

1. Peel the parsnips. Roughly chop them into 1-inch rounds and set aside.

2. Heat the butter in a saucepan. Add the parsnips and allow them to brown slightly.

3. Pour enough cool filtered water into the pot to just cover the parsnips. Add the salt and thyme spring and cover the pot with a tight-fitting lid.

4. Turn the heat to high, bring the mixture to a boil, remove the lid, and then lower the heat. Allow the parsnips to simmer until very tender when pierced with a fork.

5. Using a slotted spoon, transfer the parsnips to a blender or food processor. Strain the cooking liquid into a glass measuring cup.

6. Begin blending or processing the parsnips with 1/2 cup of the cooking liquid, then slowly add more cooking liquid, about another 1/2 cup until the puree is the desired consistency.

7. The puree can be passed through a chinois or fine-meshed sieve if a smoother consistency is desired.

Twice Roasted Sweet Potatoes with Chili-Honey Butter

Yield: 4 servings as a side dish

This side dish can have many variations depending on what type of sweet potato and what type of chilies you use. When sweet potatoes are at the height of harvest season, I like to use a variety of traditional orange, purple, and Japanese white. The colors make for a stunning presentation and allow your guests to compare the flavor and texture of sweet potato varieties. Keep in mind that purple sweet potatoes will take longer to cook in the first step. While this recipe calls for a Serrano chile, you can substitute a more or less spicy variety depending on your level of heat tolerance. In the winter months, I like to use dried Calabrian chilies.

I often served these to Bruce's family with Reverse-Seared Elk or Venison as the sweetness is a great complement to the gamey meat. If you want to make these sweet potatoes vegan-friendly, you may substitute the butter with coconut oil or Miyokos brand of unsalted non-dairy butter and substitute the honey with maple syrup. It may seem odd to offer these substitutions for a dish that is frequently served with meat. We would often have vegetarian guests, so I always ensured that our meal buffets were inclusive of all dietary restrictions.

Ingredients

- 3 pounds small Sweet Potatoes, scrubbed well
- 1 Serrano chile, sliced down the middle to expose the center (remove ribs and seeds if less spice is desired)
- 4 oz grass-fed unsalted butter
- 6 oz local honey
- 1 TB freshly squeezed lime juice
- 2 tsp melted coconut oil
- Fleur de Sel, Maldon, or other coarse-finishing salt

Directions

1. Preheat the oven to 300F. Line a sheet tray with aluminum foil, then parchment paper. Poke holes in the sweet potatoes with a paring knife or skewer and bake for 40-60 minutes, turning the potatoes over halfway through. Test the sweet potato for doneness with a cake tester, toothpick, or skewer. When the potatoes are very soft, remove from the oven and allow to cool.

2. Raise the oven temperature to 425F.

3. Combine the butter, honey, and chili in a heavy-bottomed saucepan and bring to a simmer.

4. When potatoes are cool enough to handle, move them to a cutting board, discard the parchment sheet used to bake the potatoes, and replace with a fresh parchment sheet. With clean hands, pull the sharp ends from the sweet potatoes and discard them. Smash the sweet potatoes with the palm of your hand to break open the skin, then tear the potatoes into jagged bite-sized pieces. Place them skin-side down in a single layer on the parchment-lined sheet tray.

5. Discard the chili from the butter mixture. Lightly drizzle the potatoes with half of the chili honey butter mixture and bake for 15 minutes.

6. Remove from the oven and drizzle with more of the chili honey butter mixture, reserving some for serving. Return the tray to the oven for another 10-15 minutes until potatoes are browned and crispy.

7. Remove the tray from the oven. Using a fish spatula, transfer the potatoes to a serving tray. Reheat the remaining Chili-honey-butter mixture in the pot and drizzle on the potatoes. Just before serving, finish with lime juice, melted coconut oil, and a few generous pinches of coarse salt.

8. Serve and watch your guests swoon.

Chapter 16
Renzo Gracie Academy
The Blue Basement and Açaí

It should shock no one that billionaires live with abduction and death threats hanging over their heads on a daily basis. Danger follows money, and money hires protection. My travels as a private chef brought me into the orbit of some remarkable individuals—former soldiers, cops, and Special Forces badasses who had swapped combat zones for the discreet world of private security. For them, it was still a battlefield—only now the food was better, and they got to trade fatigues for crisp linen shirts with better food. I've always had immense respect for those who wear—or once wore—a uniform: the quiet guardians who keep chaos at bay so the rest of us can breathe easy.

In 2013, I flew to the Caribbean several days ahead of my principals 'holiday trip to grocery shop, stock the kitchen, and start prep. One night over dinner with the estate managers and the SecOps team, we got into a conversation about the global uptick in violent crime. I admitted to the guys—both former Navy SEALs—that I often felt uneasy walking alone in New York City at night. I asked if there was a martial art I could learn to make me feel less like a victim.

They answered in unison: "Brazilian Jiu-Jitsu."

One of them grinned and said, "Train BJJ for six months, and you'll be able to kick our asses."

I was sold.

Descent into the Blue Basement

Brazilian Jiu-Jitsu (BJJ) is a grappling-based martial art that emphasizes leverage, technique, and strategy over brute strength. Adapted from traditional Japanese Jiu-Jitsu and Judo, the Gracie family refined it in Brazil to allow smaller fighters to control and submit larger opponents using joint locks and strangles. It's not just a physical discipline—it's mental, philosophical, and endlessly humbling.

When I got back to New York, I enrolled at Renzo Gracie Academy. Truthfully, I had no idea who Renzo was—or what I was about to get myself into.

You reached the academy by descending a narrow staircase off 30th Street, down into what everyone called "The Blue Basement." The name fit. The mats were royal blue, the air thick with humidity and the sharp tang of sweat and disinfectant. The moment you hit the bottom step, the place hit you back—bodies colliding, the slap of palms on mats, the thud of takedowns, coaches barking commands in English, Portuguese, and the universal language of grit.

It wasn't glamorous. It wasn't sanitized. It was pure Jiu-Jitsu—raw, hard-core, and oddly welcoming. Lawyers rolled with cops. Bouncers sparred with bankers. Anyone could walk in off the street and share the mat with world champions.

I told myself I'd train for six months, just enough to feel stronger—or at least to back up my big talk to the Navy SEALs.

What I didn't know was that walking down those stairs would become the single most transformative step of my adult life.

The Kitchen and the Mats

To my surprise, success in martial arts mirrored success in kitchens. Both demanded the same relentless repetition—the same refusal to take shortcuts. You show up every day, whether you feel like it or not, and you do the work until it becomes second nature.

When I was at Gramercy Tavern, I was assigned two cases of tomatoes every morning to blanch, peel, deseed, and tray for tomato confit. The first day, it took me hours. A month later, I could finish in record time without losing precision, because every morning I competed against myself.

When I started training at Renzo's, I applied that same mentality. The first time I tried to "shrimp"—a fundamental movement in Jiu-Jitsu—I looked like a flipped beetle struggling to right itself. By the end of the month, I was keeping up with higher belts. Today, I can hip-escape almost as smoothly as I peel a carrot.

Fuel and Fire

During my years competing in Jiu-Jitsu tournaments, my diet—and my clients 'diets—changed dramatically. I was nearly forty, often facing women in their twenties. To keep up, I had to train smarter, recover faster, and fuel myself properly.

I'd been a lightweight rower in college. Staying "light" had always been a fight. I figured out through painful trial and error what foods gave me power without weighing me down. My partner and I even won the New York State Collegiate Rowing Championship in 1999.

Naturally, I thought that same diet would carry me through Jiu-Jitsu two decades later. Big mistake. Oars don't try to strangle you. The energy dump after rolling was brutal, and I had no idea how to refuel.

That changed when I joined the Gracie family for a week-long Jiu-Jitsu camp in Playa del Carmen, Mexico.

The Açaí Revelation

The Gracies were everything I expected: fierce, disciplined, and full of life. Roger, Rolles, Gregor, Igor, Daniel—all of them moved like human panthers and ate like monks. I watched closely as their plates filled with fruits, vegetables, lean proteins, cheeses, and slow-burning carbs like oats and rice. When they invited me to sit with them, I did what I always do—I asked about food.

At the time, I had a small side hustle called Tembatoo Granola, selling a few hundred bags a week at Hamptons farm stands. I'd brought some with me to Mexico to snack on and share.

When the Gracies tried it, they all agreed it would make an amazing açaí bowl.

I blinked. "What's an açaí bowl?"

The table erupted in laughter and disbelief. Rolles—declared the "açaí bowl master"—took it upon himself to educate me. He described the process with such detail that when I got home to New York, I nailed it on my first try.

Soon, açaí bowls became my post-training ritual. They replenished my energy and became a full-blown obsession. I interrogated every Brazilian at Renzo's for their secrets until I had it down to a science. Before long, my apartment turned into a breakfast café after morning class—me in my gi, whipping up bowls for my training partners.

Breakfast with Renzo

One morning, Master Renzo himself showed up. He usually trained in the afternoons, but that day he was at the academy early for belt promotions. The guys were already coming to my place for breakfast, and Renzo decided to join.

Suddenly, I was terrified. Making an açaí bowl for Renzo Gracie felt like cooking rice for the Chinese consulate—something I'd actually done, and been equally nervous about.

Renzo is impossible to be nervous around for long. He radiates warmth, generosity, and joy. His energy fills a room. When he took the first bite, he grinned and said, "Best açaí bowl of my life."

I exhaled for the first time all morning.

Within minutes, my living room rug turned into a Jiu-Jitsu mat. Renzo and the crew were demonstrating moves between the coffee table and couch. Renzo is to Jiu-Jitsu what a great chef is to cuisine—a master technician who lives and breathes his craft and shares it freely.

Oysters and Brotherhood

When I started cutting weight for competitions, I discovered my perfect fuel: oysters. Low in calories, high in protein, loaded with zinc—oysters kept me lean, strong, and healthy while training twice a day. After long sessions on the mats, I'd meet my Jiu-Jitsu brother, Max McGarr, Renzo's right-hand man and the academy's manager, for dozens of raw oysters at The John Dory.

There was something poetic about it—slurping cold, briny oysters after a night of sweat and grind in the Blue Basement. The sea in its purest form; recovery distilled to a single bite. When we were in heavy competition training, the oysters were our reward—clean fuel for tired bodies and clearer minds. But when we weren't in fight camp, those oysters were just the opening act. They were followed by copious pints of beer, tequila, and long, rowdy nights with Renzo, Max, and the crew—laughing, talking technique, solving life one round at a time. Surrounded by trained killers with hearts of gold, I never felt safer walking the streets of New York.

No one ever messed with us. It was our version of a post-service kitchen hang. The tribe was the same; the uniforms just swapped whites for gis.

Tony and the Mats

Through Jiu-Jitsu, I also formed a friendship with Chef Anthony Bourdain. I'd first met his wife, Ottavia, before Tony started training. She was—and remains—one of the fiercest women I've ever rolled with.

When Tony caught the BJJ bug, we were both white belts. During the summers, he and Ottavia rented a home in Southampton, and we trained under the Vamos Brothers in Holbrook, NY—black belts under Joe D'Arce, who earned his from Renzo himself. Neither of us wanted to be labeled a creonte (Portuguese for "traitor") by training outside the Gracie lineage, so Vamos became our second home.

The hour-long drive there and back became sacred time. We talked about food, about fighting, about life. Those conversations—equal parts philosophy and profanity—are ones I wish we could still have.

Training felt like an extension of our work in kitchens. Both demanded the same thing: focus, presence, and problem-solving under extreme stress.

Ottavia once wore a shirt that read, "Jiu-Jitsu Makes Us Equal."

I didn't fully understand it until the day Tony and I walked onto the mats together.

When Tony entered any room, he was a celebrity. But when he tied his belt and stepped onto the mats, he was just another lanky, middle-aged guy with a lot of heart and zero ego.

The mats don't care who you are—how rich or poor, how famous or unknown. The mats only care that you show up. Some days you're the hammer. Some days you're the nail. Every roll is a fight for your life.

That kind of work—the sweat, the pressure, the constant edge of survival—it turns down the volume on all of life's noise.

Jiu-Jitsu couldn't save Tony. But it gave him moments of peace, and a tribe that loved him fiercely.

I miss him. I'm grateful for the meals we shared, for the conversations, and for the sweat we left behind together in The Blue Basement at Renzo Gracie Academy.

Reflection

The kitchen taught me discipline; the mats taught me humility. Both demanded everything—time, patience, pain, and passion. In the kitchen, I learned to control chaos with precision. On the mats, I learned to surrender to it and breathe through the storm.

Between the sweat, the oysters, the açaí, and the sound of bare feet squeaking across blue vinyl, I discovered that mastery—of food, of movement, of self—isn't about domination. It's about flow.

Some days you're the hammer; some days you're the nail. But whether in the kitchen or on the mat, the goal remains the same: never stop rolling.

Dana & Master Renzo Gracie (photo credit Dan Behr)

Jiu Jitsu training with Tony

Me nervously making my first açaí bowl for Master Renzo and Professor Zed in 2014

Açaí Bowl

Yield: 2 servings

A properly made açaí bowl should have the consistency of raspberry sorbet. It takes a few tries and a little patience to master the technique in the blender, but once you get it right, you will easily execute it every time. I often let the frozen ingredients sit in the blender for a few minutes to make them easier to process, but you want to be careful not to let them completely unfreeze, or you will be serving açaí soup.

Ingredients

- 8 oz unsweetened frozen açaí chunks
- 1 oz frozen wild blueberries
- ¼ tsp grated fresh ginger
- 4 oz unsweetened tart cherry juice
- 1 scoop grass-fed collagen powder (optional)
- 1 oz pure maple syrup (optional)
- 3 oz granola
- 1 medium ripe banana, peeled and diced
- Runny honey for drizzling overtop (optional)

Directions

1. Place two cereal bowls in the freezer.

2. Place the frozen açaí, wild blueberries, ginger, and half of the tart cherry juice in a blender pitcher. Begin to pulse the blender on low speed, breaking up the açaí. Turn the blender off, remove the lid, and scrape down the sides of the blender with a wooden spoon or spatula.

3. Add the remaining tart cherry juice and pulse the blender on low speed, increasing the speed to medium-high, turning the blender off and scraping down the sides as necessary. When the mixture is

homogeneous and looks like sorbet, add the maple syrup and collagen powder (if using)

4.   Remove the cereal bowls from the freezer. Divide the açaí mixture between the two bowls. Top with the granola and diced bananas. Drizzle honey over the bowl if desired and serve immediately.

Pickled Horseradish for Raw Shucked Oysters on the Half-Shell

Yield: 1 pint

Fresh oysters are a nutritional powerhouse. Regular consumption of oysters (2-3 times/ week) keeps my clients and me healthy and sniffle-free all winter. Oysters are a phenomenal option for fighters cutting weight as they are low in calories, high in protein, and extremely abundant in Zinc, vitamin B12, and copper- all minerals that keep the body healthy during cold and flu season. I like to serve raw shucked oysters with pickled horseradish- another great source of antioxidants. I make one large batch of pickled horseradish in late October when horseradish comes into season and serve it throughout the winter with shucked raw oysters.

Ingredients

- 1 large horseradish root (about 1 pound)
- 1 tsp kosher-sized sea salt
- 2 cups champagne or white wine vinegar
- Agrumato lemon olive oil

Directions

1. Rinse the horseradish under lukewarm running water to remove any excessive dirt, then submerge the horseradish root in warm water and allow it to sit for 30 minutes.

2. Remove the horseradish from the water and scrub well with a vegetable brush running with lukewarm water to remove any remaining dirt.

3. Cut the horseradish into 2-3 inch pieces for ease of handling. Carefully remove the skin with a sharp paring knife or y-shaped vegetable peeler. Rinse the horseradish one more time with lukewarm water.

4.   Using the fine-shred side of a box grater or a fine shred disc of a food processor, shred the horseradish. Transfer to a non-reactive bowl or container (glass is preferable). Sprinkle the salt over the horseradish, then pour the vinegar over the horseradish until it is just submerged. Allow the mixture to sit, uncovered and unrefrigerated, overnight.

5.   The next day, drain the horseradish, reserving 1 cup of the vinegar. Place the drained horseradish in the bowl of a food processor with the standard blade. Process for 2 minutes, scraping down the sides of the bowl as necessary.

6.   With the food processor running, slowly pour in the reserved 1 cup of vinegar, then the Agrumato lemon oil, and process until fully combined. Add salt to taste. If the flavor is to your liking, transfer the pickled horseradish to a mason jar and refrigerate.

7.   If the pickled horseradish is too pungent for your taste, allow it to sit an extra day at room temperature before transferring it to a mason jar.

8.   Store the pickled horseradish in a glass mason jar and refrigerate for up to 6 months.

Chapter 17
Green Acres 2.0

I had been living what most people would consider a dream: a great Manhattan apartment with my soon-to-be husband, Brice, and our two full-grown Rhodesian Ridgebacks. Brice's middle daughter, Tyler, stayed with us on occasion while she worked in the baking department at Eataly's Flatiron location just across the street. Our apartment, about a thousand square feet, was palatial by New York standards. We were steps from the Madison Square Park dog run— city life at its most civilized. We had rhythm, comfort, and a skyline outside our window.

For a decade, I'd been feeding my neighbors on those same park benches—people who had nowhere else to go. I brought them leftovers, hot meals, socks, coats, books, and dignity. The two homeless women who lived near the fountain always got boxes of tampons and pads. We knew one another by name and by ritual. "Morning." "Afternoon." "Evening." It was our quiet community in the city that never slept.

But by 2017, the neighborhood began to change. The faces in the park weren't familiar anymore. Many were mentally unstable, and their behavior was unpredictable. One man's favorite pastime was chasing women through the park with his pants around his knees. I watched him get arrested one morning, only to see him back at it the next day.

Then came the needles. I'd pass men and women openly shooting up along 26th Street—morning, noon, and night. Even with my Jiu Jitsu training, one hundred seventy pounds of lion-hunting canine, and a six-foot-six former rodeo cowboy by my side, I no longer felt safe walking home after dark.

At the time, I was working mostly Monday through Thursday in the city. Bruce Wayne—my long-time client—had built a kitchen in his midtown office just for me, where I prepared his lunches and consulted on menus for his global properties. It was fulfilling, but I was feeling the grind. The trains began to look less like a commute and more like a path to freedom.

A Lone Tree and a New Life

Brice saw it too. Quietly, he started looking for farms in the Hudson Valley, knowing my dream had always been to restore an old barn and build a farm-to-table venue—a place where I could feed people honest food surrounded by open air and stars.

He proposed at a Dierks Bentley concert, just as "Thank God for This Woman, Amen" hit its last chorus. We eloped in Central Park, packed up the dogs, and bought fifty acres of rolling farmland in Warwick, New York—complete with century-old red dairy barns and a sweeping view of the valley.

We named it Lone Tree Farms, after the lone shagbark hickory standing tall on the hilltop. The name was also a nod to Brice's Texas roots—one lone tree for the Lone Star. Every season, that tree stood watch over us, its silhouette framed by snow, wildflowers, or late-summer sun.

The barns, though beautiful, were tired and sagging. The former owner, Mr. Capone—a character straight out of small-town Americana—was aging and had long since stopped hosting his grand gatherings in the old banquet hall. Most people looked at the property and saw decay. We saw potential.

We skipped the honeymoon, poured cocktails, and spent our evenings riding the tractor—our "land boat"—to the hilltop, charting plans for crops and livestock under watercolor sunsets. We were giddy, delirious, and completely out of our minds.

The First Feast

That fall, my new husband and I hosted a farm-warming wedding celebration on the anniversary of the night we met. It was pure country magic: pulled pork, mac and cheese, cornbread, and kale Caesar salad under strings of lights. Our daughters, family, and friends pitched in.

One of my Jiu Jitsu buddies, a black belt turned blacksmith, made firepits from metal barrels. My stepdaughter lined the paths with paper-bag lanterns, and guests rode hay wagons to the top of the hill for s'mores under the stars.

It was our first successful event—and proof that we were meant to build something real together.

Momentum and the Moment Everything Stopped

We spent that winter renovating. By February 2020, the early thaw brought a sense of momentum and possibility. I commuted to the city, and Brice managed the farm work—grading roads, building fences, restoring ponds. Our social media posts drew inquiries for weddings. The calendar started to fill.

Then, March arrived. And the world stopped.

The pandemic ripped through New York like a silent bomb. Restaurants shuttered overnight. Chefs—people who lived to serve—were suddenly told that their work, their craft, their purpose, was "nonessential." The entire hospitality industry fell to its knees.

We would have welcomed a pause, but there's no such thing as time off when you own a farm. Calves don't wait for lockdown to end. Our Scottish Highland cattle were due in April, which meant we needed fencing—immediately.

When a meddling neighbor reported us for "nonessential work," we were forced to stop. I couldn't believe it. Fencing, to feed and contain livestock, was deemed nonessential. (Spoiler: beef comes from cows, cows need fences, fences are essential.)

The New York State Department of Agriculture eventually agreed, but we lost precious days, money, and patience.

The Call from Bruce Wayne

And that's when Bruce Wayne called.

He wanted me back. He was moving his family to one of his remote estates and wanted to ensure their health during lockdown. His longtime chef wasn't cutting it. He offered triple my salary to return—temporarily—to cook for the family. Brice and I agreed. The farm could wait; this opportunity would help fund its growth.

I became the only person allowed to leave the estate grounds. I shopped at local farms, sourcing nutrient-dense foods, and built menus designed to strengthen immune systems and keep everyone thriving. One of the barns had been converted into a gym, and I started training CrossFit at 4 a.m. with the estate manager. We were living proof that wellness comes from work, fresh air, and real food—not fear.

By May, I was driving home on my days off to find Brice transforming our dream into reality. He'd built patios, hung string lights, and turned our barns into something straight out of a Southern Living spread. Livestock now grazed across the pastures—Scottish Highlands, horses, pigs, ducks, and the inevitable farm dog brigade.

What was meant to be a few weeks away stretched into five months. When I finally returned full-time in September, I was exhausted, but the farm was blooming.

A City Gone Silent

Manhattan, though, was hollow. The heartbeat of the city—the restaurants, theaters, and crowded sidewalks—had gone eerily quiet. Times Square was empty. The lights still burned, but no one was there to see them. The soul of hospitality had been gutted.

When the vaccine rolled out, it was first offered, then required. Despite everything I'd sacrificed—months away from my husband, working nonstop to keep others well—I was told I'd lose my job if I didn't comply. My doctor advised against it for personal medical reasons, but my autonomy wasn't up for negotiation.

The Last Stand

I walked away.

For years, I'd been flexible to a fault—adapting to others' whims, schedules, and tastes. But this was different. Health is personal. Freedom is nonnegotiable. And no paycheck—no matter how large—was worth surrendering either.

So Brice and I sold the farm, packed up our lives, and drove south to Texas—back to his roots and toward something freer. We brought the truck, the dogs, and our beloved potbelly pig, Tuna- our own real life country song.

We left behind fifty acres of blood, sweat, and dream dust. But we carried with us what mattered most: resilience, experience, and the unshakable knowledge that true sustenance—whether from food, work, or life itself—comes only when it's rooted in freedom.

Photo credit: Christopher Sutcliffe from "Outstanding in the Field" August 31, 2024 Springs Fireplace Farm. Cornbread cooked in mini muffin tins to serve a crowd of 180 guests.

Dana's Cornbread

Yield: 8 servings

Ingredients

- 1 cup medium grind cornmeal
- ¾ cups AP flour (or GF flour)
- 1.5 tsp baking powder
- ½ tsp baking soda
- ½ tsp salt
- 5 TB melted butter
- 1 TB melted bacon fat
- ⅓ cup honey
- 2 eggs, beaten
- 1-½ cups buttermilk

Directions

1. Preheat the oven to 425 degrees. Butter a cast iron skillet or dark metal baking dish.

2. Place dry ingredients in a large bowl and whisk until homogenous.

2. In a separate bowl, combine wet ingredients and whisk until homogenous and emulsified.

3. Mix the wet ingredients into the dry ingredients.

4. Pour the batter into the prepared pan and bake for 20-25 minutes until the top is golden brown and a toothpick inserted into the center comes out clean.

Pulled Chicken

Yield: 4 servings

This chicken can be made on a charcoal grill, gas grill, or even in the oven. If you do not plan to use a grill, I recommend making the southern dry rub with smoked paprika instead of traditional sweet paprika to impart a smoky flavor.

Ingredients

- 2 pounds organic chicken thighs, skin on, bone-in
- ½ cup Southern Dry Rub (recipe follows)
- ¼ -½ cup North Carolina-style BBQ sauce (recipe follows)

Directions

1. Season both sides of the chicken thighs generously with the Southern dry rub. Place in a glass baking dish, cover, and refrigerate overnight.

2. Take the chicken out of the fridge to bring it to room temperature. Light a gas or charcoal grill to a low temperature, around 300°F. Grill the chicken, skin side down, for 20-30 minutes, or until an instant-read thermometer registers 165°F when inserted into the thickest part of the thigh.

3. Allow the chicken to rest for at least ten minutes. When the chicken is cool enough to handle, begin pulling it off the bone into shreds. Save the bones to simmer into a bone broth if desired.

4. Slowly drizzle in ¼ cup of the BBQ sauce and mix well. If a more piquant vinegar flavor is desired, add the rest of the BBQ sauce. Serve the pulled chicken with warm cornbread, biscuits, or in lettuce cups if you are avoiding carbs.

Southern Dry Rub

Yield: 2 cups

This dry rub is indispensable for my pulled pork and chicken. It is also a great seasoning for grilled chicken, pork chops, and vegetables.

Ingredients

¼ cup packed brown sugar

½ cup sweet or hot paprika

¼ cup chili powder

2 tablespoons ground red pepper

2 tablespoons ground cumin

1/2 tsp ground allspice

¼ cup salt

¼ cup cracked black peppercorns

Directions

1. Whisk all ingredients together in a bowl until they become homogeneous. Store in an airtight container until ready to use, up to 6 months in a cool, dark place.

North Carolina BBQ Sauce

Yield: 1-½ cups

Ingredients

*   ¾ cup white wine vinegar
*   ¾ cup apple cider vinegar
*   1 TB crushed red pepper flakes
*   1 TB runny honey
*   Salt and cracked black pepper to taste

Directions

1. Whisk all ingredients together in a bowl until homogenous. Store in an airtight container for up to six months

Tuscan Kale Caesar Salad (with the addition of poached eggs and crispy capers for a hearty lunch salad)

Tuscan Kale Caesar Salad

Yield: 6 servings

I do not use eggs in my Caesar dressing. Instead, I utilize a little extra Dijon mustard, which helps to emulsify the dressing. I also do not add cheese to the dressing itself since I am often serving guests with multiple dietary restrictions. Instead, I fold the cheese into the salad when I am mixing in the dressing, and when I have a dairy-free guest joining a dinner party, I simply omit the cheese from the guest's portion.

Ingredients

For the Greens

• 2 bunches washed Tuscan kale (also called lacinato or dinosaur kale)

• 1 TB Agrumato lemon olive oil

• A few pinches of kosher-sized sea salt

For the Dressing

• 4 oil-packed anchovy filets

• 1 clove of fresh garlic

• 1.5 TB Dijon mustard

• 2 TB freshly squeezed lemon juice

• ⅓ cup extra virgin olive oil

• 2 TB Agrumato lemon olive oil

• 1 tsp freshly ground black pepper

For The Topping

• 1 cup organic panko breadcrumbs

• 1 TB extra virgin olive oil

• Pinch of sea salt

• 4 oz grated parmigiano-reggiano

Directions

1. Cut out the center rib from each kale leaf. Roughly chop the kale into bite-sized pieces and place it in a large bowl. Add the Agrumato oil and salt to the greens and massage them into the kale with clean hands. Set aside.

2. Preheat the oven to 350°F. Place the panko breadcrumbs in a bowl. Add the extra virgin olive oil and salt. Mix well. Spread the breadcrumbs out onto a parchment-lined sheet tray. Bake the bread crumbs until they are golden brown, 8-10 minutes. Remove from the oven, allow to cool, and transfer to a bowl.

3. Make the dressing: place the anchovy filets, clove of garlic, Dijon mustard, and lemon juice into the pitcher of a blender. Blend until homogenous.

4. With the blender running on low, slowly drizzle in the extra virgin olive oil in a thin stream. As the dressing begins to emulsify, slowly add the remaining olive oil, then the lemon oil, then the freshly ground black pepper.

5. Assemble the salad: sprinkle half of the parmigiano-reggiano onto the massaged kale. Add the dressing, ¼ cup at a time, and mix well until the desired dressing amount has been added.

6. Divide the salad among six salad plates. Top with the remaining Parmigiano-Reggiano, then the toasted breadcrumbs, and serve.

7. This salad can be prepared several hours in advance up to step 6, then finished with the additional cheese and breadcrumbs when ready to serve.

Chapter 18
God Bless Texas!

In June of 2021, my husband and I sold our farm, packed our lives into a truck, loaded up our dogs and pig, and headed south to Austin, Texas. The world was still shaking off the aftermath of lockdowns, but for us, it was a clean start.

My first order of business was to find the farms—the heart of any food community. I combed through every lead, searching for the best markets, the hidden growers, the kindred spirits who lived for soil and sun. My search, however, was unfruitful.

Austin's restaurant economy had been pummeled. The music festivals that drove so much of the city's foot traffic had vanished overnight in 2020. The rodeo—canceled. Dozens of beloved local restaurants never reopened. And when they fell, their farmers fell with them. The largest supplier to Austin's independent restaurants went under.

That story echoed all over America. Chefs, farmers, and restaurateurs—people who feed their communities—were forced to forfeit their livelihoods. The average restaurant profit margin is only three to five percent. That's $2.50 profit on a $50 entrée. When you take away the ability to open the doors, you take away survival itself.

Learning to Cook in a Land That Doesn't Want to Grow

Texas, I quickly learned, is not an easy place to farm. The soil is alkaline, the rain unpredictable, and the summer heat feels like opening the door to a blast furnace. Unlike the Northeast, where summer is one endless harvest, Austin farms shut down for survival. Nothing can grow when the earth feels like it's breathing fire.

Still, I found my rhythm. Freelance jobs trickled in—dinner parties, private events, and eventually a big one: a fifty-person dinner and private concert downtown. The headliner was none other than Jack Ingram, a true Texas music legend.

The day was long, hot, and beautiful chaos. My husband and I, with the help of a local chef named Kacey, executed an upscale Tex-Mex menu for the event. When the kitchen was spotless and the last plate cleared, the host invited me to the bar to share a drink with him and Jack Ingram. I was still in my chef coat, hair damp with sweat, but when a Texas icon offers whiskey, you say yes.

That night, I finally exhaled. I was a chef in a new city, and I'd just pulled off my first real Austin event.

Starting Over

The gigs slowed after that. I didn't have the deep connections in Austin that I'd built over decades in New York. I swallowed my pride and registered with staffing agencies, knowing I might have to start from scratch.

By then, the Silicon Valley migration had begun. Elon Musk had arrived. Joe Rogan was giving Americans permission to question everything. The tide was turning, and I knew that eventually, opportunity would follow money—as it always does.

But in the meantime, I took a 70% pay cut and accepted work that barely covered the bills. I cooked for families who treated staff as accessories to their status. After years working for "Bruce Wayne"—a billionaire who embodied grace, intellect, and genuine decency—this was humbling, and often infuriating.

My client's constant need for social climbing was exhausting. I cooked for people who bragged about friendships they didn't have and name-dropped connections that weren't real. Ironically, I later cooked for the very high-powered people they claimed to know—and learned that those "friends" had long since stopped accepting their invitations.

Still, I did what chefs do: I put my head down and cooked my heart out. No matter who sat at the table, the food always deserved respect.

Rooting Myself in Texas Soil

Eventually, I found my footing. Through trial, error, and persistence, I discovered a handful of good small farms that operated during the cooler months—places like Buda Botanicals in Buda, TX, and Boggy Creek Farm in East Austin.

I learned the local rhythms. Up north, I'd mourn the last fresh tomatoes in November. In Texas, I was pulling heirlooms in January. My menus began to shift with the landscape.

One thing never changed: the presence of beef. Texans raise a lot of it—and they raise it beautifully. I cooked more beef in a single year than I had in the previous five combined. Reverse-seared ribeyes, marinated skirt steak fajitas, dry-aged strips on the Big Green Egg—each dish kissed with smoke and fire.

But I left the brisket to the masters. Competing with Franklin BBQ, Terry Black's, or Leroy and Lewis would've been culinary blasphemy. There's a sacred art to Texas barbecue, and I respected it enough to simply admire it.

Returning to the Hamptons

When my first Austin job ended in late spring, I caught wind of opportunities back in my old Hamptons stomping grounds. The summer season was ramping up, and the idea of escaping the Texas heat was irresistible.

Back in Water Mill, I felt like I'd stepped into a cool ocean breeze. I walked through The Green Thumb Organic Farm, inhaling the scent of sun-warmed herbs and just-pulled carrots. The Hamptons, for me, has never been about glitz. It's about the purity of ingredients—the rhythm of fishermen, farmers, and food lovers coexisting on a narrow stretch of land.

During the lockdowns, those relationships had saved me. When grocery store shelves went bare, my farmers still delivered. When the world panicked, they just kept growing.

One evening during those long months, I'd stumbled across a recipe for Peruvian Roast Chicken. Instead of roasting it whole, I spatchcocked the bird, saving the backbone for stock. The sauce was traditionally mayo-based, but since my clients loathed mayonnaise, I swapped it for coconut cream. The result was vibrant, spicy, and luscious—a hit from the first bite.

So when I cooked for my Hamptons client that summer, I made that dish. After dinner, his longtime housekeeper, Amaryllis, came back to the kitchen grinning.

"Mr. K is loving your chicken!"

I peeked out and saw him, sauce smeared across his plate, grinning like a kid.

He looked up, fork still in hand, and said, "Dana... this chicken... it's just epic."

From that night forward, the dish was renamed Mr. K's Chicken. It became my signature—equal parts comfort, craft, and care.

Don't California My Texas

When I returned to Austin later that year, I stepped into a very different role: Executive Chef to one of the new Silicon Valley transplants. The salary matched my experience, and the mission matched my heart—build a culinary program from the ground up, one that balanced performance, longevity, and flavor.

Unlike the established East Coast estates, this family was just forming their household staff. I hired two sous chefs and several contract cooks, building a team that worked like a well-tuned line.

We traveled constantly—Napa, LA, Aspen, New York, back to Austin. Often times in the same couple of weeks.. In Aspen, we made après-ski charcuterie spreads and perfected hot chocolate that could make an Olympian weak at the knees. In summer, we grilled Paonia peaches and mixed salads with herbs from the farmers' market.

In Austin, our days revolved around health-forward food and meticulous menu planning. Once again, I worked with Dr. Peter Attia's medical team, fine-tuning the family's nutrition with surgical precision. We created a rhythm that balanced clean eating with joy—because even billionaires need cheat days.

Friday nights meant homemade pizza on the Big Green Egg. Sunday mornings were for pancakes—big, fluffy buttermilk ones that never lasted long enough to cool.

Cooking for tech billionaires was a different beast entirely. Of course we did massive levels of entertaining. Large, glamorous outdoor events, children's parties, board dinners, family holidays. But during the day-to-day-, it was often difficult to find a rhythm. There were no formal mealtimes, no family table. Meals were served on trays, eaten in front of glowing screens, ordered through Slack or WhatsApp. Everything was fast, flexible, efficient. Food as fuel.

It wasn't my style, but it was the new world—and I adapted.

Mr. K's Chicken

Yield: 8 servings

Ingredients

For the Chicken

- 2 whole chickens
- 1 whole lemon, quartered for rubbing the chicken
- 8 cloves fresh garlic, peeled
- 2 TB toasted cumin seeds
- 2 TB XVOO
- 1 TB Agrumato lemon oil
- 2 TB paprika (substitute smoked paprika if making in the oven and not on a grill)
- 1 tsp black pepper
- 1 tsp dried oregano
- 1 tsp kosher salt
- ¼ cup fresh lemon juice
- 2 tsp kosher salt for seasoning the bird before grilling

For the Tangy Green Coconut Sauce

- 4 scallions with green tops, roughly chopped
- 2 cups packed cilantro with tender stems
- 1 cup mint leaves
- 2 coarsely chopped jalapeños
- 2 TB XVOO
- 1 fresh kaffir lime leaf (or 1 tsp lime zest)
- 5 tsp freshly squeezed lime juice
- ½ tsp salt
- ⅔ cup coconut cream

Directions

1. Preheat a gas or charcoal grill to 300°F.

2. Place the chickens, breast side down, onto a work surface. Using kitchen shears, cut along both sides of the backbone to spatchcock the chicken. Remove the backbone and reserve it to make bone broth or chicken stock.

3. Turn the chicken over, breast side up, and press on the center of the breastbone until you hear it crack and the chicken is laying flat. Rub the entire chicken with the juice side of the quartered lemons. Discard the lemons.

4. Place the garlic, cumin seeds, both olive oils, paprika, black pepper, oregano, 1 tsp kosher salt, and 1/4 cup of lemon juice in the pitcher of a blender. Purée the ingredients into a fine paste. Transfer to a small bowl.

5. Loosen the skin from the chicken on both edges of the cavity, taking care not to rip the skin. Using your fingers, stuff the spice paste under the skin of the chicken breast, thighs and legs.

6. Season the chickens with the remaining salt. Scrub the grill grates well with a grill brush, then wipe the grates with oil to keep the chicken from sticking. Place the chicken on the grill, skin side down, taking care not to burn the chicken skin.

7. After 10-15 minutes, utilizing two large flat spatulas, shimmy the spatulas under the chicken being careful not to tear the skin, and turn the chicken 45 degrees to create grill marks on the chicken skin. After another 10-15 minutes, carefully flip the chicken over, breast side up, and continue cooking the chicken until the internal temperature reaches 165°F on an instant-read thermometer inserted into the thickest part of the chicken.

8. While the chicken is cooking, prepare the green sauce. Place the scallions, cilantro, mint, lime leaf (or lime zest), jalapeños, extra virgin olive oil, lime juice, and salt into the pitcher of a blender.

Pulse until ingredients are combined, then puree to form a smooth paste. Add the coconut cream and puree the mixture until smooth. Transfer to a serving bowl.

9. When the chicken has finished cooking, transfer it to a rack-lined sheet tray and allow it to rest for 15 minutes.

10. Carve the chicken and serve with the tangy green sauce.

If you have the budget, invest in a mica clay pot for cooking your bean dishes. This vessel imparts a unique flavor that enhances the depth of the beans.

Charro Beans

Yield: serves 10 as a side dish

Whenever I make "Mr. K's Chicken", I make broth with the leftover carcasses. I discovered that using this broth in the charro beans makes for an especially tasty version. The broth is easy. Put the carcasses in a pot, pour in enough water to cover the bones by 4 inches, and simmer for 4 hours, season to taste, and strain.

Ingredients

- 1 pound dried pinto beans
- kosher-sized sea salt or fleur de sel as needed
- 6 cups (1.5 qt) homemade or store-bought low-sodium chicken stock
- 2 bay leaves
- 2 sprigs epazote (optional)
- 12 ounces nitrate-free diced hardwood smoked bacon
- 1 medium onion, diced (about 1 cup)
- 2 serrano chiles or one jalapeño, minced (remove seeds and ribs if you prefer less heat)
- 3 medium cloves garlic, grated on a rasp grater
- 2 (14-ounce; 400g) cans diced fire-roasted tomatoes (or 32 oz fresh Roma tomatoes if they are in season, lightly charred and pureed)
- Zest of 1 lime (no bitter white pith)
- Juice of 1 lime (about 1 oz or to taste)
- ½ cup chopped cilantro leaves and stems

Directions

1. Place beans in a large vessel and fill with enough cold filtered water to cover by at least four inches (if you have a Kangen

machine, use the 9.5pH setting). Add two tablespoons (18g) salt and stir to dissolve. Let soak for 8 to 12 hours. Drain and rinse.

2.   In a Dutch oven, add beans, stock, bay leaves, 2 teaspoons (6g) kosher salt, and epazote (if using). Bring to a boil over high heat, reduce to a very low simmer, cover, and cook until beans are just tender, about 45 minutes.

3.   Meanwhile, place bacon in a cold 12-inch stainless steel or cast iron skillet, then bring up to medium-high heat. Cook, stirring constantly, with a wooden spoon until fat is rendered and bacon is just starting to brown around the edges, about 5 minutes. Add onion and chiles and cook, stirring with a wooden spoon, until softened and just starting to brown, about 4 minutes. Add garlic and cook, stirring, until fragrant, about 30 seconds. Add tomatoes and cook, stirring and scraping up browned bits from the bottom of the pan, until the liquid is thick and the mixture begins to sizzle, a few minutes more.

4.   Remove the lid from the Dutch oven, and add the bacon-tomato mixture and lime zest. Continue cooking, stirring occasionally, until the beans are completely creamy and the liquid has thickened, this can take anywhere from 20-40 minutes. It should look like a rich, creamy broth and the beans should be tender and creamy.

5.   Season to taste with salt and lime juice. Discard bay leaves, stir in cilantro, and serve. Beans can be stored in the refrigerator for up to 1 week or cooled and frozen for up to six months.

Pizza cooked on the Big Green Egg.

Chef Dana's Signature Pizza

Yield: 4 pizzas

This pizza utilizes Jim Lahey's no-knead pizza dough recipe. I have successfully made this pizza at the high altitude of Aspen, CO, at sea level in The Hamptons, and in the Hill Country of Texas. An accurate-to-the-gram digital scale is needed for making the dough.

There is one made by Escali, available on the Ample Kitchen website: https://amplekitchen.com

You can add toppings to this pizza as desired. Just keep them light so it doesn't weigh down the light, airy, and crispy pizza.

Dough Ingredients

- 500g 00 Pizza flour, plus more for shaping the dough
- 1g Active Dry Yeast
- 16g Fine Sea Salt
- 350g Filtered Water (I prefer Kangen 9.5)

Pizza Topping Ingredients

- 1 14 oz can of Whole Peeled San Marzano Tomatoes
- 1 clove of fresh garlic
- 2 whole leaves of fresh basil
- 12 leaves of fresh basil, torn into smaller pieces
- ¼ tsp sea salt
- 1 TB Extra virgin olive oil plus more for drizzling
- 12 oz fresh cow's milk mozzarella, drained, cut into 1/4's and sliced
- 4 oz grated Parmigiano-Reggiano

Dough Directions

1. In a medium bowl, whisk together the flour, yeast, and salt until well combined. Add the water and mix with a wooden spoon until the mixture is thoroughly combined.

2.   Cover the bowl with a kitchen towel, lid, plate, or plastic wrap. Allow the dough to rise at room temperature (72°F) for 18 hours or until it has more than doubled in size. If the room is warm, the time will be shorter. If the room is cold, the time will be longer.

3.   Flour a work surface and scrape the dough out of the bowl, onto the floured work surface.

4.   Divide the dough into 4 equal portions using a bench scraper or floured knife.

5.   Shape the dough: for each portion, start with the right side of the dough. Pull it away toward the right, then up toward you, and fold it over to the center of the dough. Do the same with the left, top, and bottom sides. The order is not important, you are just creating four folds in the dough.

6.   Place each portion seam-side down, shape each portion into a round, and then return to the floured board, seam-side down. The mounds should not feel sticky. If they are, dust them with a bit more flour.

7.   If you don't plan to use the dough immediately, the balls can be wrapped individually in plastic and refrigerated for up to 3 days. Return to room temperature by leaving them out on the counter for 2-3 hours before needed.

Pizza Directions

1.   Set a baking stone in your oven. Preheat the oven to 525°F. Alternately, prepare a Komodo-style charcoal grill like the Big Green Egg and follow the manufacturer's instructions for making pizza.

2.   Strain the juice from the can of tomatoes and reserve it for another purpose. Place the strained tomatoes in a blender with the clove of garlic, 2 whole basil leaves, and ¼ tsp of sea salt. Blend until thoroughly combined. Pour into a vessel that can easily fit a small ladle and set aside.

3. Stretch a ball of the pizza dough into a twelve-inch circle. Lightly flour a pizza peel and place the dough on the pizza peel. If you would like the pizza to be thinner, you can roll the dough with a floured rolling pin. Be sure that the dough is not sticking to the peel.

4. Ladle 1/4 of the tomato sauce into the center of the pizza, then spread it lightly in a circular motion using the bottom of the ladle, using care not to press too hard on the dough and leave the rim of the pizza without sauce.

5. Sprinkle 1 oz of the Parmigiano-Reggiano over the pizza. Evenly arrange 3 leaves worth of the torn basil over the tomato sauce and parmigiano-reggiano. Place 1 slice of the fresh mozzarella over each piece of basil.

6. Carefully slide the pizza from the pizza peel onto the hot pizza stone. Allow to bake for 7-8 minutes in the oven, rotating the pizza halfway through the cooking process. When the crust is crisp and the cheese is bubbling, remove the pizza from the oven. Allow it to rest a minute or two before slicing.

7. Repeat the process with the remaining three pizzas.

Cooked on a griddle, the pancakes are softer and fluffier on the edges.

Cooked in a cast iron skillet, the pancakes are light and fluffy on the inside with a pronounced crunchy brown edge.

Fluffy Brown Butter Buttermilk Pancakes

Yield: 4 to 6 servings

The addition of Greek yogurt to these pancakes gives them an extra boost of protein. When cooking for clients on cheat days, as per Dr. Attia's medical team, I needed to hit client protein targets and this addition made it possible without compromising on flavor. If you do not want to use Greek yogurt, you can substitute it with the same amount by weight of buttermilk, sour cream, or creme fraiche.

Ingredients

- 10 (about 2 cups) ounces Organic all-purpose flour
- 1-¼ tsp aluminum-free baking powder
- ½ tsp baking soda
- 1 TB organic sugar
- 1 tsp kosher-sized sea salt
- 2 large eggs, separated
- 12 oz organic buttermilk
- 8 oz full-fat organic Greek yogurt
- 2 tsp pure vanilla extract
- 4TB unsalted butter plus more for serving
- Clarified butter or ghee for cooking the pancakes
- Warm maple syrup for serving

Directions

1. Whisk together the dry ingredients: flour, baking powder, baking soda, sugar, and sea salt together in a large bowl until thoroughly combined and set aside.

2. Melt the 4 TB butter in a small saucepan on low heat. Once the butter is melted, increase the heat to medium-high and simmer, stirring with a wooden spoon, until the butter hisses and pops.

Continue cooking and stirring until the butter is golden brown, scraping up any browned bits as you go along. Strain the butter into a small bowl and allow it to cool slightly.

3. Using a very clean whisk and a clean bowl, whisk the egg whites to soft peaks and set aside.

4. In a large bowl, whisk together the egg yolks, buttermilk, Greek yogurt, and vanilla extract until homogenous. Drizzle in the butter and whisk well.

5. Pour the wet ingredients into the bowl with dry ingredients and fold together until just combined. The mixture should remain a bit lumpy. Fold in the egg whites until just combined, again, allowing the mixture to remain slightly lumpy.

6. Heat a large, heavy-bottomed cast iron skillet or griddle. Add a small amount of clarified butter or ghee to the pan and spread it around in a thin layer.

7. Using a ¼ cup measure, place 2-4 pancakes into the skillet (depending on the size of your skillet). Allow to cook over medium heat until bubbles begin to form on the top and the bottoms are golden brown, about 2-3 minutes. Flip the pancakes over and allow to cook for 2-3 minutes on the other side until the pancakes are cooked through. Repeat the process with the remaining batter.

8. Serve the pancakes warm with plenty of soft butter and maple syrup.

Chapter 19
The Importance of Flexibility

One of the greatest keys to success in the private chef world is flexibility — not just in body or schedule, but in mindset. If you can't adapt, you won't survive.

Working for billionaires means being able to pivot at any moment: menus change, guests arrive unannounced, and dietary restrictions appear out of thin air. The ability to accommodate food allergies and personal preferences without flinching is what separates the professionals from the amateurs.

Among my clients and their high-society circles in New York, there's a curious trend: an outright aversion to raw alliums. Garlic, in particular, is a repeat offender. Chives and scallions might squeak by, but raw garlic is often met with a hard "no."

The trick, of course, is never letting it throw you off balance — even when you find out at the eleventh hour.

I vividly remember a summer luncheon in the Hamptons for a well-known billionaire fashion designer. Fifty guests, a lavish buffet, fifteen dishes — my team and I had been working since dawn. The table was a canvas of color and texture: grains, greens, seafood, salads, and every farmer's market gem I could get my hands on.

Just minutes before service, the hostess appeared in the kitchen with one of her guests. "Chef, I'd love for you to meet my friend," she said. He smiled politely, leaned in, and said, "By the way, I'm vegan."

"No worries," I said, scanning my mental menu. "We have a quinoa sal—"

He interrupted. "I also don't eat grains."

Now, I've seen chefs crumble in moments like this — roll their eyes, throw a tantrum, mutter something unprintable under their breath. I've always believed that our job as chefs isn't to feed egos; it's to feed people. So instead of reacting, I smiled and said, "Sir, we'll make sure you have a delicious meal."

I took a quick inventory of what we had prepped and spotted the solution. I whipped up a lemon-tahini sauce, folded it into some organic beans — yes, from a can, because every good chef keeps them for exactly this reason — then tossed in roasted vegetables and herbs from the day's prep. Within minutes, we had a bright, balanced, beautiful dish that fit every one of his dietary needs.

After lunch, the guest returned to the kitchen with the hostess, both smiling. He thanked me sincerely, saying he rarely eats at events because most chefs either can't or won't accommodate him. His gratitude was genuine — the kind that stays with you.

A few days later, a package arrived. Inside was a stunning piece from his personal fashion collection, a token of appreciation. But for me, the real reward was that moment in the kitchen — knowing I'd given someone the simple joy of being included.

In this world, where opulence often overshadows empathy, small acts of care stand out the most. Sometimes the mark of a great chef isn't what's on the menu — it's how gracefully you handle what isn't.

Lemon-Tahini Sauce as part of a seasonal vegetable grazing board.

Tahini sauce served with grilled chicken skewers.

Lemon Tahini Sauce

Yield: about 2 cups

Depending on my client's tastes, I either make this with scallions, raw garlic, or garlic confit. The raw garlic will be the most pungent, the garlic confit being the gentlest. Each brand of tahini has a different consistency, so you may need to add more water than specified here to keep your blender from seizing up.

This sauce is great on everything from grilled meats and fish to vegetables.

Ingredients

- 2 cloves of garlic (or 2 scallions, sliced or 4 cloves of garlic confit- recipe follows)
- ½ cup freshly squeezed lemon juice
- 1 small jalapeño, ribs and seeds removed
- 2 tsp kosher-sized sea salt plus more if needed to taste
- 1 cup of tahini paste
- 1 tsp ground cumin
- ½ tsp smoked paprika
- ½ cup cool filtered water or more as needed
- 1 TB Agrumato lemon olive oil
- 1 tsp unrefined toasted sesame oil
- ¼ cup Italian Parsley leaves

Directions

1. Place garlic, scallions, or garlic confit in the pitcher of a blender. Add the fresh lemon juice, jalapeño, and salt. Pulse the blender until a loose puree is formed.

2. Add the tahini paste, cumin, smoked paprika, half a cup of water, lemon oil, and toasted sesame oil. Pulse to puree into a smooth paste, adding more water as necessary to keep the blender

running smoothly. Add the parsley and puree again until very smooth. Season to taste. Store in an airtight container in the refrigerator for up to 10 days.

Garlic Confit

Yield: 1 pint

Garlic confit is a great way to get allium flavor into dishes without the pungent bite of raw garlic. Many of my UHNW clients choose to avoid anything with strong garlic or onion flavor as the scent can linger on the breath (and for some, out of the pores when they sweat). Slowly cooking the garlic at a low temperature in extra virgin olive oil removes the sharpness of the garlic, making it sweet and spreadable, and eliminating the uncomfortable garlic breath when socializing in intimate settings. The garlic-flavored oil that sits on top can be used in many preparations, including salad dressings, mixing into marinated olives, and drizzling over soups, pasta, or even grilled meats, fish, and vegetables.

Ingredients

- 2 whole heads of garlic
- 1-½ cups extra virgin olive oil (or more if needed)

Directions

1.   Preheat the oven to 250°F. Separate the garlic cloves, trim off the root end, and peel each clove of garlic.

2.   Place the garlic into a small saucepan and add enough extra virgin olive oil to completely submerge the garlic.

3.   Set the pan over medium heat. You do not want to fry the garlic. Once you see small bubbles forming, remove the pan from the heat and place it in the low oven.

4.   Slowly cook the garlic in the oil for 45 minutes- 2 hours, depending on the size of the garlic cloves and the amount of heat your oven puts out. Check the oven every 20-30 minutes to ensure the garlic is not frying.

5.   The garlic confit is done when the cloves are pale golden and easily pierced with a knife. When it has finished cooking, transfer

the garlic and oil into a glass mason jar and let it cool in the fridge with the lid off. Once the confit is very cold and the extra virgin olive oil has become more solid, cover the container with a tight-fitting lid. Use the garlic confit within 2-3 weeks.

Baked Beluga Lentil Falafel
Yield: 10-12 lentil falafels

I love falafel. Unfortunately, I have a chickpea sensitivity that does not allow me to eat them. As it turns out, many of my clients have the same sensitivity. I developed this lentil falafel for that reason. You can make these with any type of lentil. I choose the black beluga lentils for my clients because they are higher in protein than other lentil varieties. This recipe works with chickpeas if you prefer them, but the soaking time will be a bit longer since chickpeas are larger than lentils.

You can deep-fry these falafel, but I like to keep my clients ' diets clean. Therefore, this recipe calls for shaping the falafel in a ring mold (fancy name for a set of round cookie cutters), brushing it with olive oil, and baking it. These are fantastic with tahini sauce and a simple Israeli salad with lots of fresh mint.

Ingredients
- 1 cup dried beluga (black) lentils
- Filtered water as needed
- ½ medium-sized onion, diced
- 1 clove of garlic, peeled and sliced
- Leaves from 4 sprigs of fresh parsley
- 1 tsp kosher-sized sea salt
- 1 tsp smoked paprika
- ½ tsp cardamom
- 1 tsp ground cumin
- 1 tsp ground coriander
- 1 Serrano or jalapeño chili, seeded and minced
- 1 tsp baking soda
- Extra virgin olive oil, as needed

- Lemon wedges for serving

Directions

1. Sort through the lentils and remove any foreign matter from them. Gently rinse the lentils, place them in a wide mouth 32 oz mason jar, and pour enough filtered water into the jar to cover the lentils by 2 inches. Soak, uncovered, overnight in the refrigerator.

2. The next day, preheat the oven to 375°F, preferably on convection. Remove the jar of lentils from the fridge, drain them, and place the soaked lentils in a food processor. Add 2TB fresh water to the food processor along with the remaining ingredients. Pulse until the lentils are finely ground and you have a homogeneous mixture.

3. Line a sheet tray with parchment paper and brush the sheet with olive oil. Portion the falafel into 2TB mounds and either roll between dampened hands to form a ball or shape them in a ring mold. Place the falafel on the sheet tray, leaving ample space between each falafel.

4. Brush each falafel with extra virgin olive oil. Bake the falafel for 10 minutes or until set. Flip the falafel over and bake for another 10-15 minutes until the falafels are crunchy on the outside and cooked through.

5. Serve warm with tahini sauce, lemon wedges, Israeli salad, and fresh pita bread.

Israeli Salad

Yield: 4-6 servings

This salad is very popular during the summer months in the Hamptons. I recommend cherry tomatoes and quartering them with a sharp knife, but really, it's best to use whatever tomatoes are ripe and local. If you use regular-sized tomatoes, just be sure to cut them the same size as the other ingredients. If you cannot find small Persian cucumbers, I recommend using Kirby cucumbers (the kind for pickling) as they are not as watery as a traditional cucumber. Just be sure to taste the skin of the Kirby cucumbers, as they can sometimes be bitter and will require peeling.

Ingredients

- 3 pints of cherry tomatoes, quartered
- 3 Persian cucumbers, cut into 1/4 inch dice
- 3 scallions, thinly sliced
- 1 jalapeño, seeded and finely minced
- 1 red or yellow bell pepper, seeded and cut into 1/4 inch dice
- 2 TB freshly squeezed lemon juice
- ½ tsp ground sumac
- 3 TB extra virgin olive oil
- ½ tsp of fleur de sel or more to taste
- ¼ cup of mint leaves, finely chopped with a sharp knife or torn into small pieces

Directions

1. Place all ingredients in a large bowl. Mix well, season to taste, and serve immediately.

Chocolate-Hazelnut Cake

Yield: 1- 8 inch cake

This cake is very Italian. Simple, not too sweet, and naturally gluten-free without using ingredients that cannot be pronounced. You can substitute almond flour in place of hazelnut flour. This cake is great on its own, but can also be served with freshly whipped cream or gelato if desired.

Ingredients

- 125 grams finely ground hazelnut flour
- 125 grams Valrhona or Mast Brothers 70% dark chocolate, chopped
- 125 grams unsalted butter, cubed
- 125 grams organic sugar
- 3 large eggs, separated
- 1 tsp pure vanilla extract
- Organic powdered sugar for dusting

Directions

1. Butter an 8-inch round springform pan and line the bottom with a circle of parchment paper. Preheat the oven to 325°F.

2. Make a Bain Marie: fill a pot with a few inches of water and place over medium heat. Place the butter in a metal or glass bowl that fits snugly on top of the pot without the bowl touching the water. Place the bowl over the pot of simmering water, allowing the butter to melt slightly. Add the chocolate and melt with the butter, stirring constantly until it is melted and homogenous. Allow the mixture to cool slightly, add the sugar and hazelnut flour.

3. When the mixture is no longer hot, stir in the egg yolks and vanilla.

4. In a clean bowl with a clean whisk, whip the egg whites to soft, fluffy peaks (you can also use a hand mixer or stand mixer).

5.   Gently fold the egg whites into the chocolate batter. Pour the batter into the prepared pan, smooth the top, and bake for 30-45 minutes. When the top appears to be dry, test the doneness using a skewer or toothpick. When inserted into the center of the cake, the skewer should come out with a few moist crumbs attached, but appear neither wet nor dry.

6.   Let the cake cool completely in the pan before unmolding, for 2-3 hours.

7.   When ready to serve, unmold the cake, dust it with powdered sugar, and serve. This cake will keep for 3-5 days at room temperature.

Chapter 20
Eating for Health

I've spent a lifetime proving what we all feel in our bones: we show love by cooking, and we sustain love by sharing a meal. But it goes further. The way to health is through food. You can't out-run, out-lift, or out-prescribe a steady diet of additives.

Clients often ask, "Is it healthy?" The honest answer: it depends on you. Some people thrive plant-forward, others animal-forward. The only diet no human can thrive on is ultra-processed food—chemical colors, lab names you can't pronounce, and a parade of "GRAS" additives dressed up as ingredients.

GRAS, in Plain English

"GRAS" means "Generally Recognized as Safe." Under the Federal Food, Drug, and Cosmetic Act, an added substance is a "food additive" requiring FDA review—unless experts agree it's safe as used, or it's been used widely since before 1958. That's the loophole. My take: "generally recognized" is not the same as "meaningfully nourishing."

When "Essential" Isn't Nourishing

COVID made our food values painfully clear. Mom-and-pop farm-to-table restaurants shuttered; drive-throughs stayed "essential." We were told to avoid sunlight, isolate indoors, and mask up—while eating factory food from a window. Visit a hospital and the cognitive dissonance gets louder: "clear liquids" arrive as fluorescent gelatin, corn-syrup broths, and bottled chemistry. Even the salad—chlorinated baby carrots, pesticide-soaked greens, seed-oil dressings—reads like a supply-chain, not a kitchen.

I keep wishing someone would film a hospital-food version of Super Size Me: one healthy adult, one month, only what's served on the tray—plus municipal tap or long-stored bottled water. We all know how that documentary ends.

Labels Lie. Ingredients Don't.

Those unpronounceable words on packages exist to extend shelf life, fake flavor, or hook your palate. We're told the chemicals are "safe in moderation," while "moderation" goes conveniently undefined. Flip the box: that's where the truth lives.

Parents, this one hurts: independent tests have found pesticide residues (including glyphosate) in mainstream cereals—the same boxes marketed as "whole grain," "heart healthy," "fortified." We're being sold reassurance on the front and reality on the back. The center aisles of the supermarket are a billboard war between brands of the same problem.

How We Got Here

We voted for it—twice. In booths, by empowering officials captured by lobbyists. And at the checkout, by buying fake food because it was easy, cheap, or cleverly labeled. No one is coming to save us. The fix is local, stubborn, and beautifully simple: buy from farmers, ranchers, and fishermen you can look in the eye.

Two bumper stickers say it best:

- KNOW FARMS KNOW FOOD (Green Thumb Organic Farm)

- DON'T BUY FOOD FROM STRANGERS (Blooming Hill Farm)

This is not a class problem. My wealthiest clients struggle to keep junk away from their kids. Those rainbow cereals? Ticking sugar bombs with dye. The "healthy" snack bars? Dessert in athletic gear. Death by a thousand cuts—and an ever-growing GRAS list.

Food as Mood (and Management)

I've watched entire offices change when the snack table changes. Grumpy bosses weren't tyrants—they were hypoglycemic. Replace candy and cookies with jars of house trail mix, spiced nuts, apple-and-peanut-butter kits (aflatoxin-tested), raw-milk cheeses with nitrate-free charcuterie, seed crackers with romesco, olives, deviled eggs made with clean mayo, jerky, lox-and-avocado tea sandwiches, beluga-lentil hummus, dark-chocolate–dipped frozen bananas (heavy-metal screened), and real smoothies—and suddenly the 3 p.m. storm becomes a breeze. Assistants stop crying. Work gets sane.

When someone's always irritable, I look at food first. Nine times out of ten, their "diet" is a parade of seed oils, dyes, and sugar disguised as fuel.

The Four Non-Negotiables

True health sits on four legs: clean air, clean water, clean food, and real sleep. Compromise one, you feel it everywhere.

Fresh Beats Shipped

A head of lettuce eaten the day it's picked is not the same as one that spent weeks on a truck, in a warehouse, and in a gas-ripening chamber. Ethylene may be "natural," but flavor and micronutrients peak on the plant, not in storage. That's why I'm relentlessly pro-farmers 'market.

Chemistry vs. Agriculture

Rainy season? Mold pressure rises. The "solution" in conventional systems is often a fungicide later flagged as a probable carcinogen—rubber-stamped by a white paper that ages poorly. We've all seen the arc: glowing study, mass adoption, class-action settlement. My answer isn't romantic—it's practical: shorten the chain. Know who grew your food and how.

Stop Blaming Food. Start Blaming What's Done to It.

Humans thrived for millennia on meat, fish, grains, legumes, fruit, honey, and nuts. The modern health collapse isn't sourdough's fault; it's processing, storage oils, chemical farming, and "fortification" by marketing department.

Healthy food doesn't need a label. At a farmstand, nothing screams "good source of." It just is.

Cost: Farmer Now or Pharma Later

I've cooked with unlimited budgets and I've cooked on a shoestring. The nutrient-dense, budget-friendly canon is ancient: rice and beans, barley and lentils, stews and curries, teff injera, the Three Sisters, small oily fish like mackerel and sardines. Real food scales. Ultra-processed doesn't nourish at any price.

If you want out—skip boxes that brag, and buy ingredients. Join a CSA. Cook. If you're intimidated, I built The Ample Kitchen Club (amplekitchen.com) to demystify it—recipes, tutorials, videos—so your family can eat like billionaires without hiring one.

The Three Ingredients I Splurge On

I don't have billionaire budgets at home. So I invest where it counts: water, fat, and salt. If these three are dirty, your health pays.

If they're clean, everything you cook gets better—flavor and biology.

Water

Water is the most abundant ingredient in any kitchen—and the most ignored. It runs through every pot, every sauce, every cell of our bodies, yet most people never stop to think about what's actually in it.

I grew up drinking water so pure it could've come straight from a fairy tale. My dad drilled a well into an underground stream beneath our Hudson Valley home, a vein of cold, living water untouched by fluoride or chlorine, rich with natural magnesium and calcium. It was crisp, mineral-kissed, and alive. I thought all water tasted that way.

Then came the yachts. Reverse osmosis became my new religion—essential when you're pulling seawater into the galley. It made the undrinkable drinkable, but it also stripped the life out of it. RO water tastes hollow, flat, almost sterile. Clean, yes. Nourishing, no.

Years later, in Manhattan, a billionaire client asked me to test the fluoride and chlorine levels at several of his properties. We collected samples from Midtown to the Upper East Side, triple-tested them, and still didn't believe the results. The levels were all over the place—sometimes far higher than what anyone should be comfortable consuming. That day, water stopped being background noise for me.

Here's the dirty secret: boiling only kills pathogens. It doesn't remove fluoride, heavy metals, or microplastics. It concentrates them. My 18-hour bone broths—so carefully tended, so nutrient-rich—would end up stronger in toxins if the water started dirty.

So I changed my entire approach. I now treat water as the first ingredient, not the last. In every kitchen I manage, I filter the incoming water to strip out the fluoride and chlorine, the invisible villains. Then I pass that clean slate through a Kangen water ionizer—a fifty-year-old Japanese technology that restructures and energizes water through platinum-coated medical-grade titanium plates. It's the difference between silence and a symphony. I've seen it reduce inflammation, boost energy, and even replace the endless parade of imported glass-bottled spring water.

The system also produces low-pH electrolyzed water—hypochlorous acid—a natural disinfectant the body itself creates to fight infection. I use it to sanitize my kitchens. No toxic residue, no artificial lemon scent, just science and nature in perfect balance.

You don't need my exact setup. But you do need to care. Test your water. Filter it. Don't assume the government's idea of "safe" matches your idea of healthy. If you live on municipal water, at the very least, start by tackling fluoride and chlorine.

Because water isn't just something you drink—it's the medium through which every nutrient, every mineral, and every cell in your body either thrives… or drowns.

Fat

The 1980s fat-phobia swapped natural fats for sugar, then for cheaper high-fructose syrup. Meanwhile, industrial seed oils—extracted with solvents, bleached, deodorized, and sometimes hydrogenated—flooded the food supply. We paid for it with our hearts and our hormones.

My kitchen fats (common sense over dogma):
- Extra-virgin olive oil: raw uses, low-temp cooking.
- Avocado oil: higher-heat sauté/roast.
- Coconut oil: when coconut flavor makes sense (and for some baking).
- Toasted sesame oil: judiciously, as a finishing flavor.

- Pasture-raised butter and ghee: flavor, fat-soluble vitamins, high-heat versatility.

- Duck fat, schmaltz, beef tallow, bacon fat: traditional, flavorful; use knowingly, with quality sourcing.

- Litmus test: if your "butter alternative" has more than two ingredients (one is salt), step away.

Salt

I avoid iodized table salt—over-processed, bleached, anti-caked. My baseline is sea salt (fleur de sel from Camargue is a favorite) and kosher-grain sea salt for brining and general seasoning. Not all salts are equal; some inland products test high in contaminants. Do a little homework and choose brands that publish testing.

If you ditch processed foods, you'll likely need to season more. That's good. Seasoning real food with clean salt is not the enemy. It's flavor—and adherence.

Organic Isn't a Trend. It's a Contract.

When people say "organic is a hoax," I invite them to cook blind with me and taste the difference. Then I show them what organic forbids that conventional allows:

Organic	Conventional
GMO's prohibited	GMO's allowed
synthetic pesticides prohibited	synthetic pesticides allowed
carcinogenic herbicides prohibited	carcinogenic herbicides allowed
toxic fungicides prohibited	toxic fungicides allowed
antibiotics and growth hormones prohibited	antibiotics and growth hormones allowed

treated municipal sewage sludge banned as fertilizer	treated municipal sewage sludge allowed to be used as fertilizer
solvents like hexane prohibited in extraction of cooking oils	solvents like hexane allowed for extraction of cooking oils
artificial petroleum-based colors prohibited	artificial petroleum-based colors allowed
builds healthy soil through centuries-old regenerative farming practices	contaminates and compacts soil through the use of industrial agricultural chemicals

And what it requires: building soil health through regenerative practices. My organic farmers are rock stars—doing what's right for bees, soil, and humans with margins that would make a banker blush. My clients pay for organic first for their health; they keep paying because the food is shockingly better.

Where This Leaves Us

If you take one thing from this book, let it be this: where you shop and what you buy is the foundation of your health.

Try this: snap a photo of your grocery basket. If 60% is packaged products with ingredient lists longer than a paragraph, expect 60% health. If you want 100%, shop like a chef: short chains, short labels, real food.

Billionaire or busy parent, the rule holds: pay the farmer now, or pay Pharma later. No one will fix this for us. But we can fix it for ourselves—one cart, one meal, one farm at a time.

Chapter 21
The Private Chef World Today

One undeniable truth about my world is that the word chef gets thrown around far too loosely. I've met plenty of domestic staff and yacht employees decked out in pristine whites who couldn't cook their way out of a paper bag—yet somehow they've convinced others to call them "chef."

Let me be clear: Chef is not an outfit. It's a title that must be earned. Just as wearing a lab coat and quoting WebMD doesn't make someone a doctor, following a recipe and plating a decent meal doesn't make someone a chef. A real chef understands the science, the discipline, the muscle memory, and the soul of cooking. It's a craft of a thousand details—each one invisible when done right.

Back in my Hamptons breakfast days, I'd run into at least five "chefs" at Citarella buying pre-marinated meats, pre-chopped vegetables, or bags of salad mix with commercial dressing. My problem wasn't the convenience—it was the lack of integrity. Why would anyone charged with feeding others 'bodies and souls willingly serve mediocrity?

When you're a private chef, your job is to know the soil, the farmers, the fishermen—to treat ingredients like language and use them fluently. You don't grab tomatoes that have traveled two thousand miles when a farm two miles away grows them in sunlight and salt air. You don't buy salad dressing. You make it.

Over the years, I've learned that many of these so-called chefs are lazy, untrained, or both. Some earn six-figure salaries cooking from boxes and cans for billionaires who never set foot in their kitchens. They fake it because they can. And their clients tolerate it because they don't know any better. The demand for private chefs has exploded faster than the supply of actual talent, and mediocrity fills the gap.

I once worked alongside a "chef" who made every baked good with Bisquick—for a billionaire with an organic garden steps from the kitchen. Meanwhile, the gardener harvested immaculate greens, washed and stored them in labeled Lexans, and this "chef" went out to buy pre-packaged lettuce instead. It was culinary malpractice dressed in starched whites.

I've never understood how someone could take that much money from a client and not care what goes into their body. If your work feeds people—literally keeps them alive—you owe them honesty. You owe them real food.

I worked my way up the hard way. No shortcuts. No faking it. I've always had kitchen morals. I cook from scratch, I honor ingredients, and I never stop learning. That's what separates a chef from a cook: when something goes wrong, we don't panic—we fix it.

A private chef's world is not glamorous; it's precision under pressure. You must be proactive, fast, graceful, and calm. You can't let a $20,000 Hermes plate slip because you're flustered. You can't scorch a sauce or raise your voice. You are expected to deliver elegance—effortlessly.

And sanitation? That's sacred. I'm an obsessive hand washer. My clients see me stop and wash my hands every time they walk into the kitchen—and that simple act earns trust. Gloves create a false sense of safety; soap and water are honest. I clean with vinegar or hypochlorous acid, never toxic sanitizers. I've cooked for billionaires for more than twenty years and have never made anyone sick. That's not luck. That's diligence.

Above all, discretion is everything. The private service world is small and gossipy, and one careless word can cost a career. I never disclose names—not to other clients, not to friends, not even on my résumé. Everyone has a code name. Everyone's privacy is sacred. You never know who's sitting at the next table, listening. And believe me, they report back. I've seen careers implode over dinner-party chatter.

I've made plenty of mistakes in my career, but I've learned from every one of them. What's carried me through is care. I care deeply about the people I feed. That's what this work demands—a heart as steady as your knife hand.

It takes patience, humility, and an ironclad sense of integrity to thrive in this business. You must care enough to say yes when it matters, to adapt when things go wrong, and to protect your clients as fiercely as you protect your craft.

I am grateful—grateful for the kitchens I've cooked in, the seas I've crossed, the farms I've stood barefoot in, and the people who've trusted me with their health.

If my story leaves you with anything, let it be this:

You don't need to be a billionaire to eat like one. You just need to care about your food, respect your body, and cook with love.

Because at the end of the day, that's all a real chef ever does—

turn raw ingredients into nourishment, and work, quietly, to make the world a little better, one plate at a time.

Epilogue
The Next Course

After decades of feeding the world's wealthiest, I've come to understand that true luxury isn't found in marble kitchens or rare caviar. It's found in clean, real food—grown with care, cooked with integrity, and shared with purpose.

That belief is the foundation of Ample Kitchen—the next chapter of my life's work. I'm building it to bring the same caliber of ingredients, technique, and intention that I've given billionaires to everyday families. Farm-to-table meals prepared with organic, seasonal ingredients. Food designed to nourish, not just impress.

My goal is simple: to make healthy eating accessible, joyful, and abundant.

Because we all deserve to eat well.

Because the kitchen is where every revolution begins.

And because feeding people—honestly, beautifully, and with love—will always be the greatest privilege of my life.